PAWS

AND

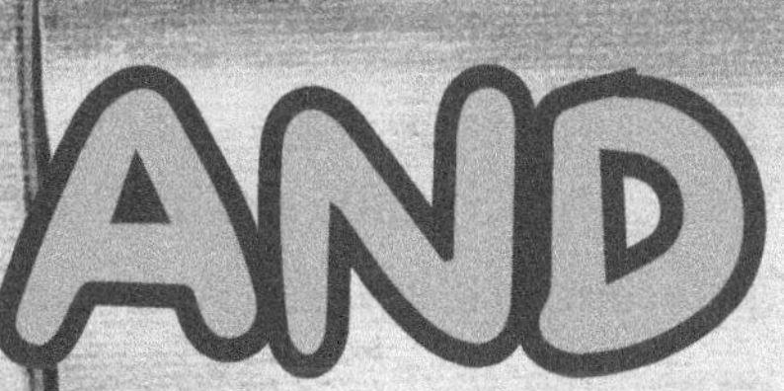

COLORS

A DOG LOVER'S COLORING ADVENTURE

Welcome to
"Paws & Colors: A Dog Lover's Coloring Adventure"

Dear Coloring Enthusiast,

Welcome to a world where creativity meets canine companionship! "Paws & Colors" is not just a coloring book. It's a heartfelt celebration of the love and beauty of dogs. Whether you're a seasoned artist or someone seeking a moment of relaxation, you've embarked on a journey that combines artistry with the joy of our four-legged friends.

Inside these pages are meticulously crafted illustrations, each portraying different dog breeds. As you bring these dogs to life with your colors, remember that each stroke is a testament to your love for these loyal and loving animals.

Let your imagination run free without limitation, and color in the most eye-catching and vibrant colors you can imagine! Dive into your coloring journey and let your creativity shine through as you artfully fill in the hues only you could bring to your project.

May this book bring you joy, tranquility, and a deeper appreciation for the furry companions who grace our lives.

So grab your favorite coloring tools, embrace art's therapeutic power, and embark on this colorful journey with friends, family, or your loyal four-legged partner!

Happy coloring!

With warm regards,

Severen Henderson

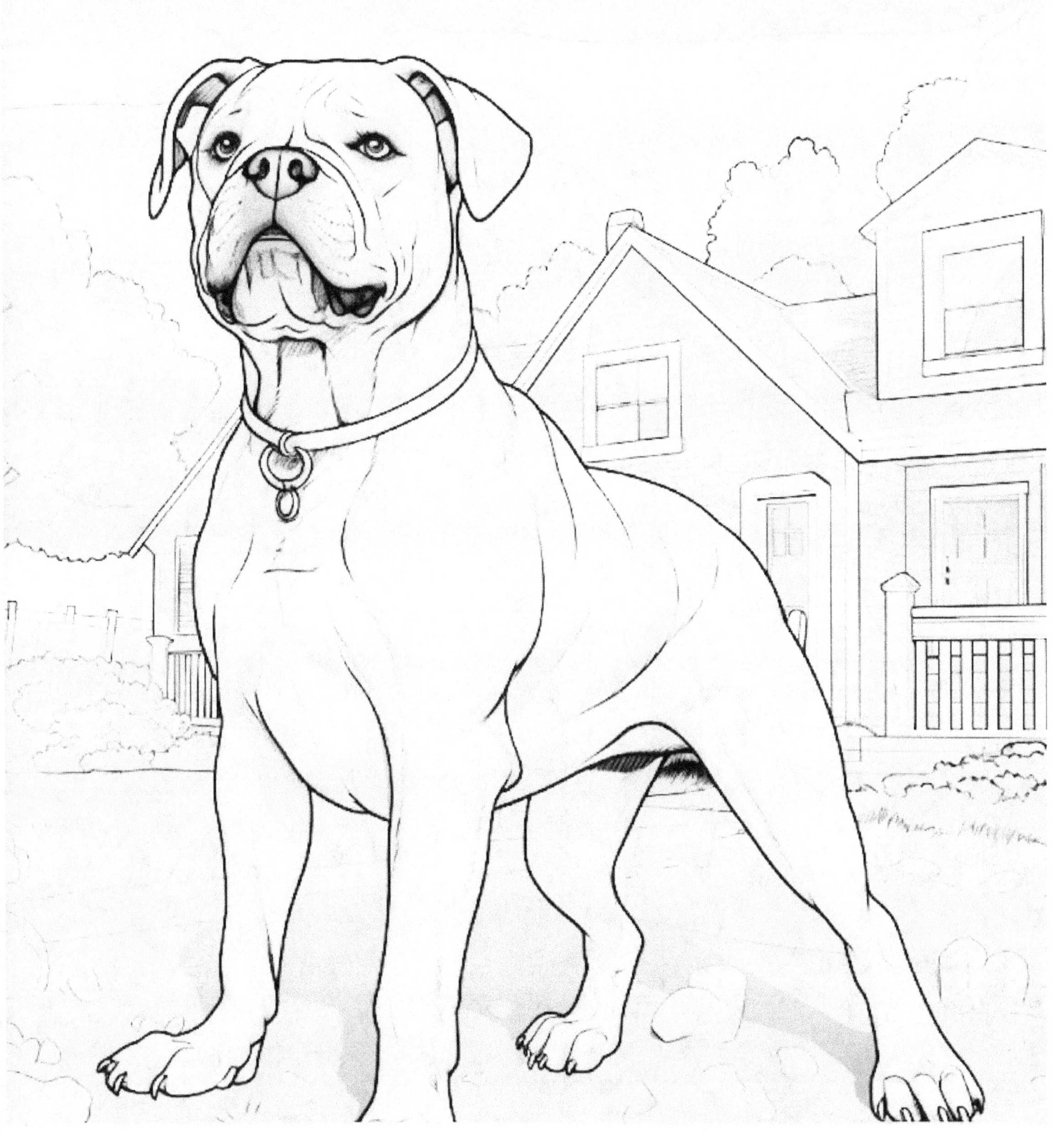

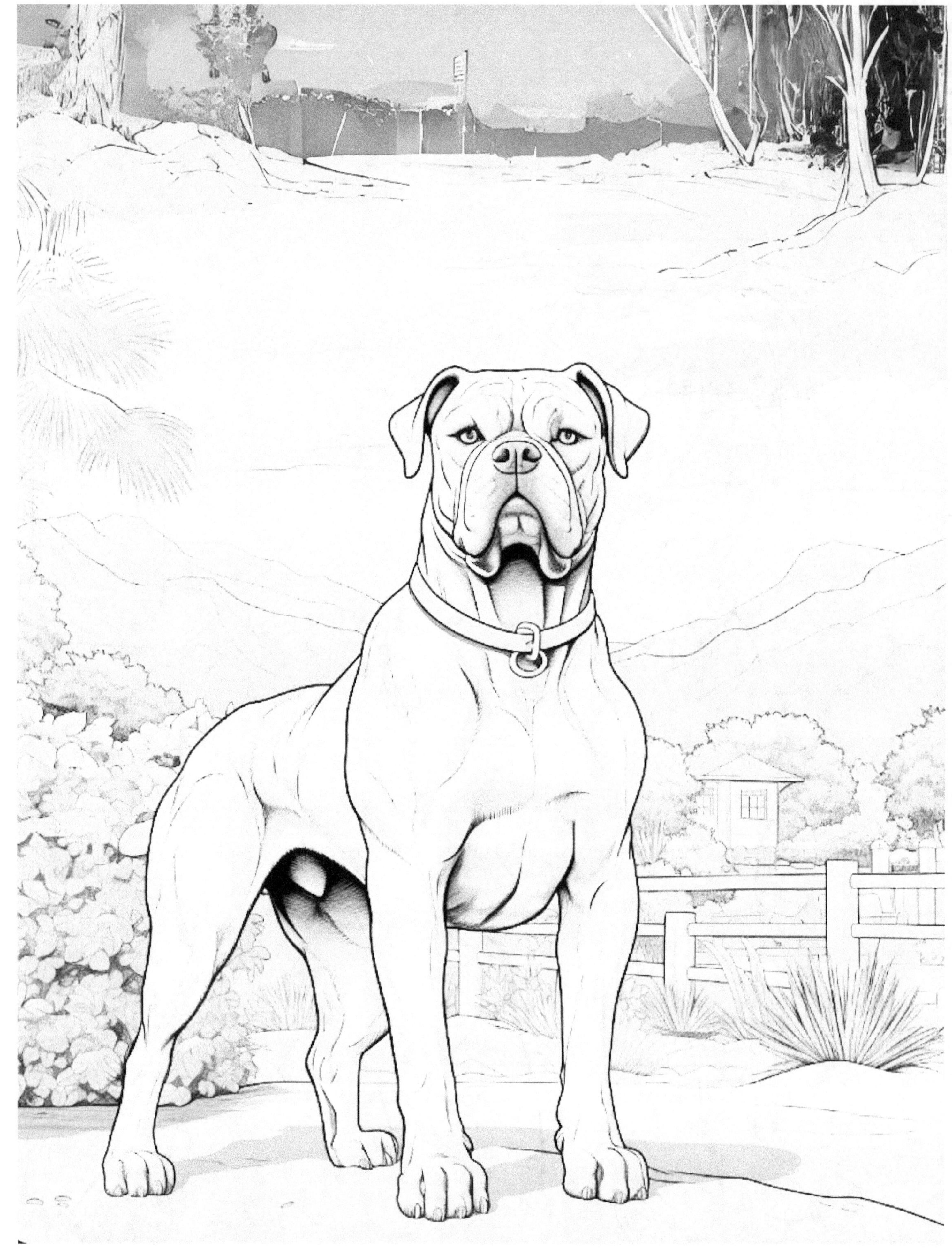

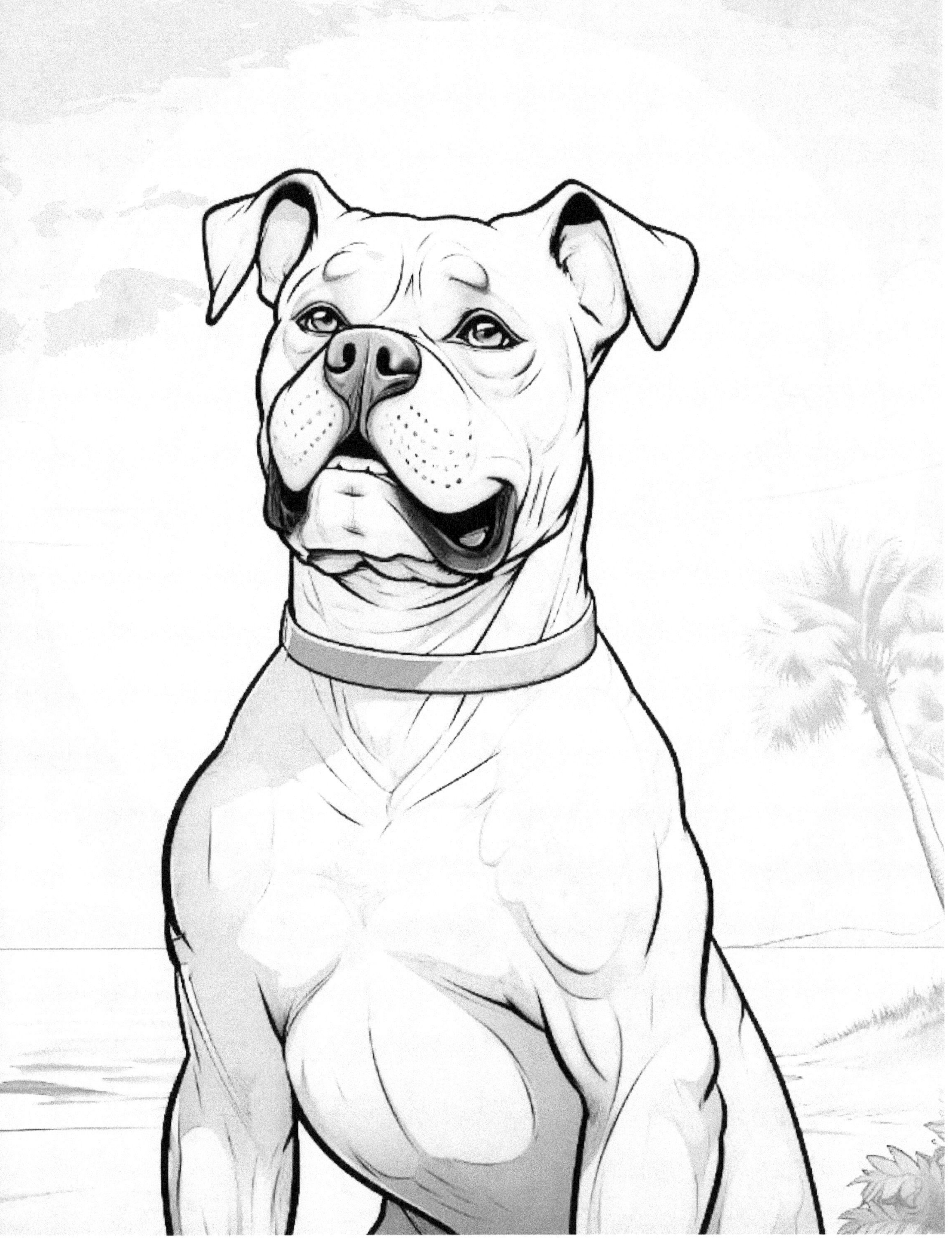

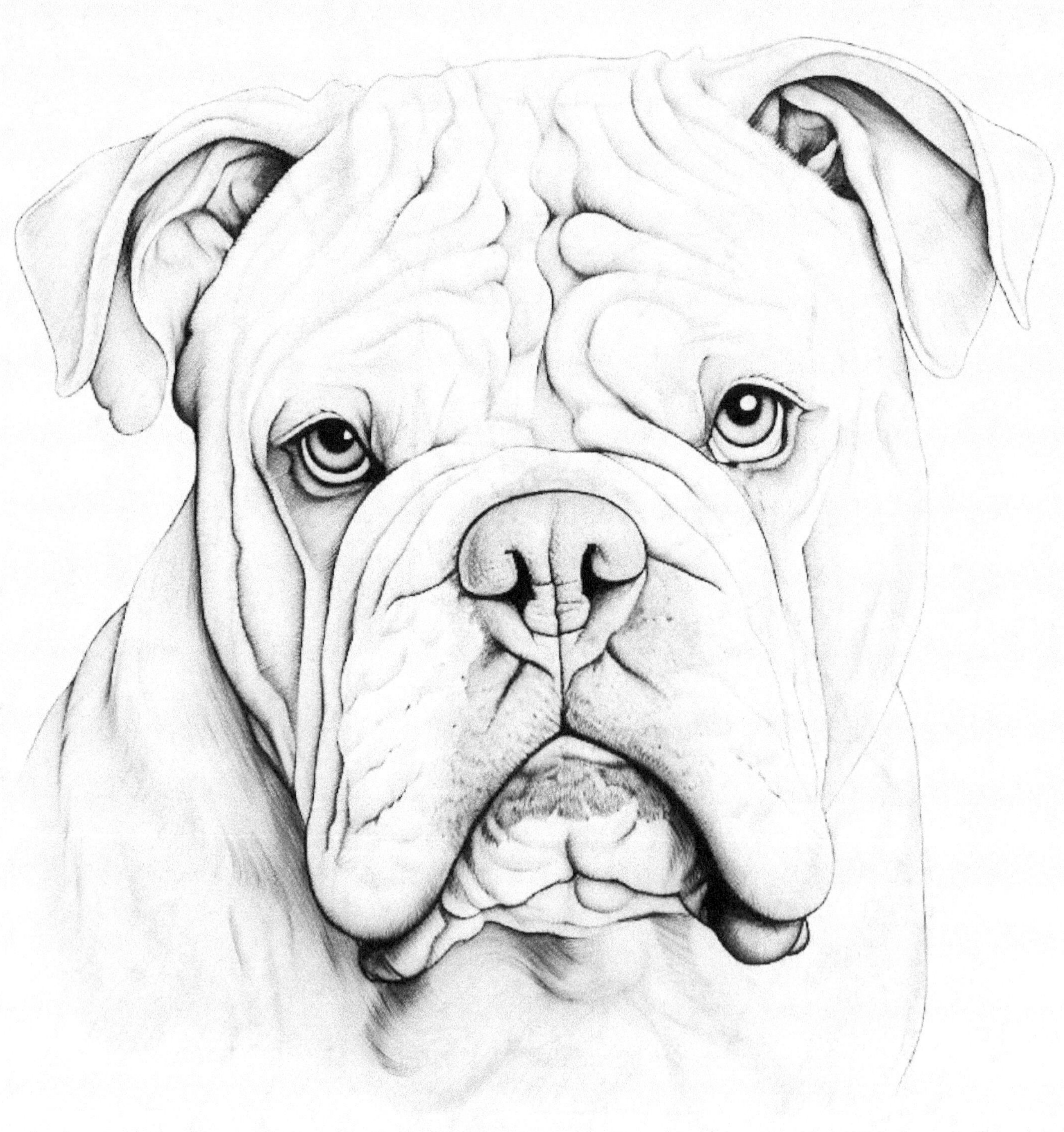

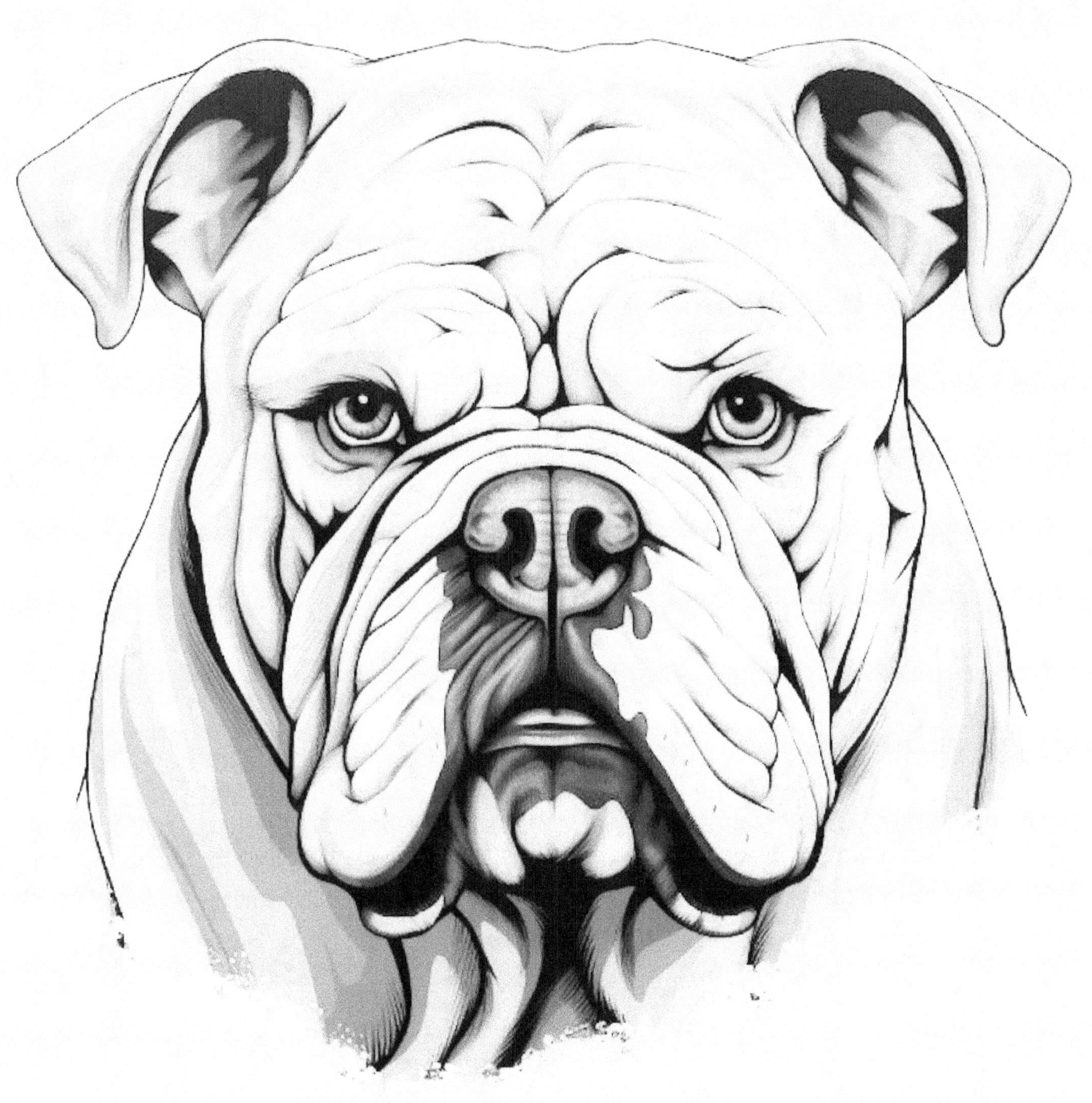

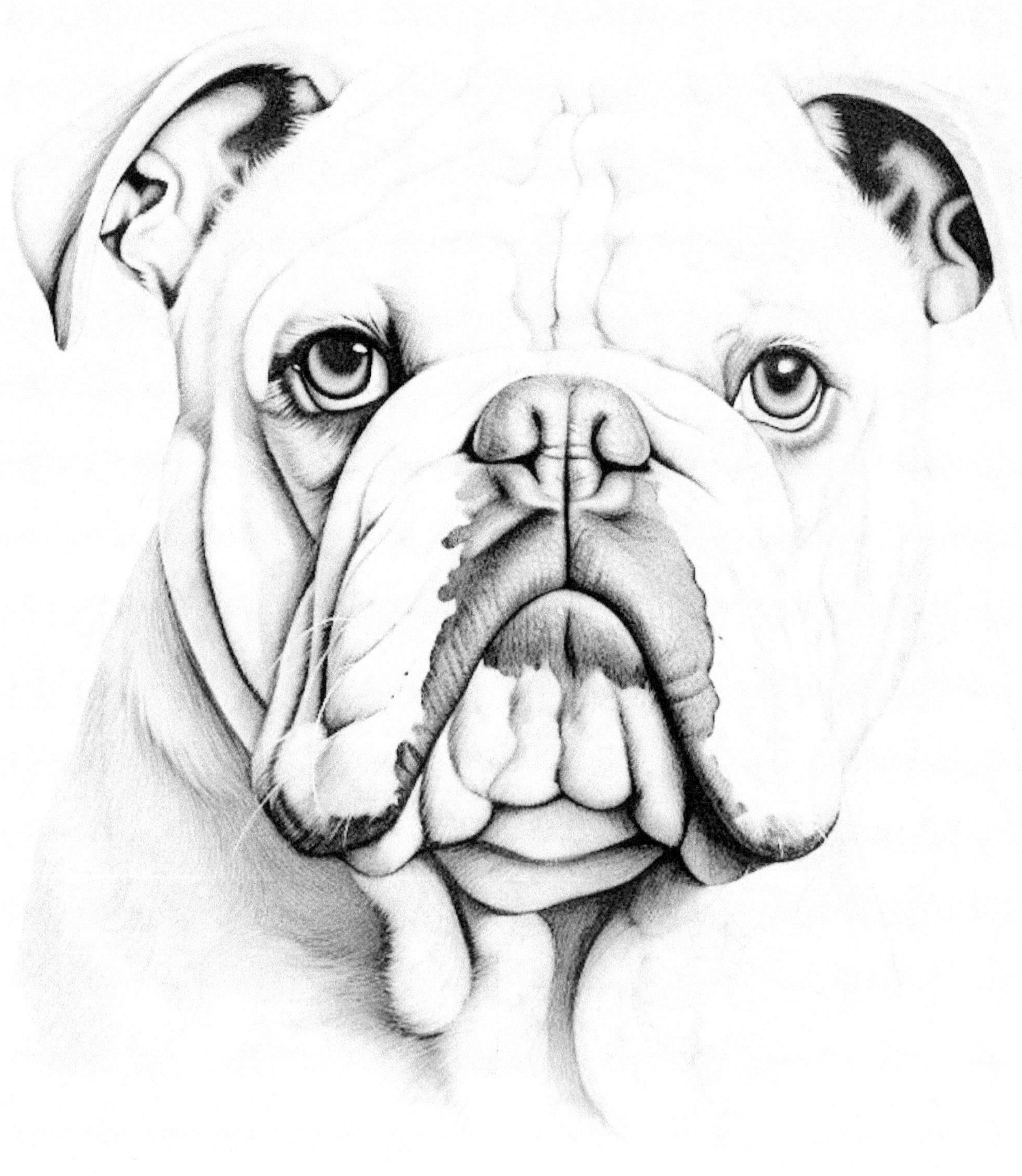

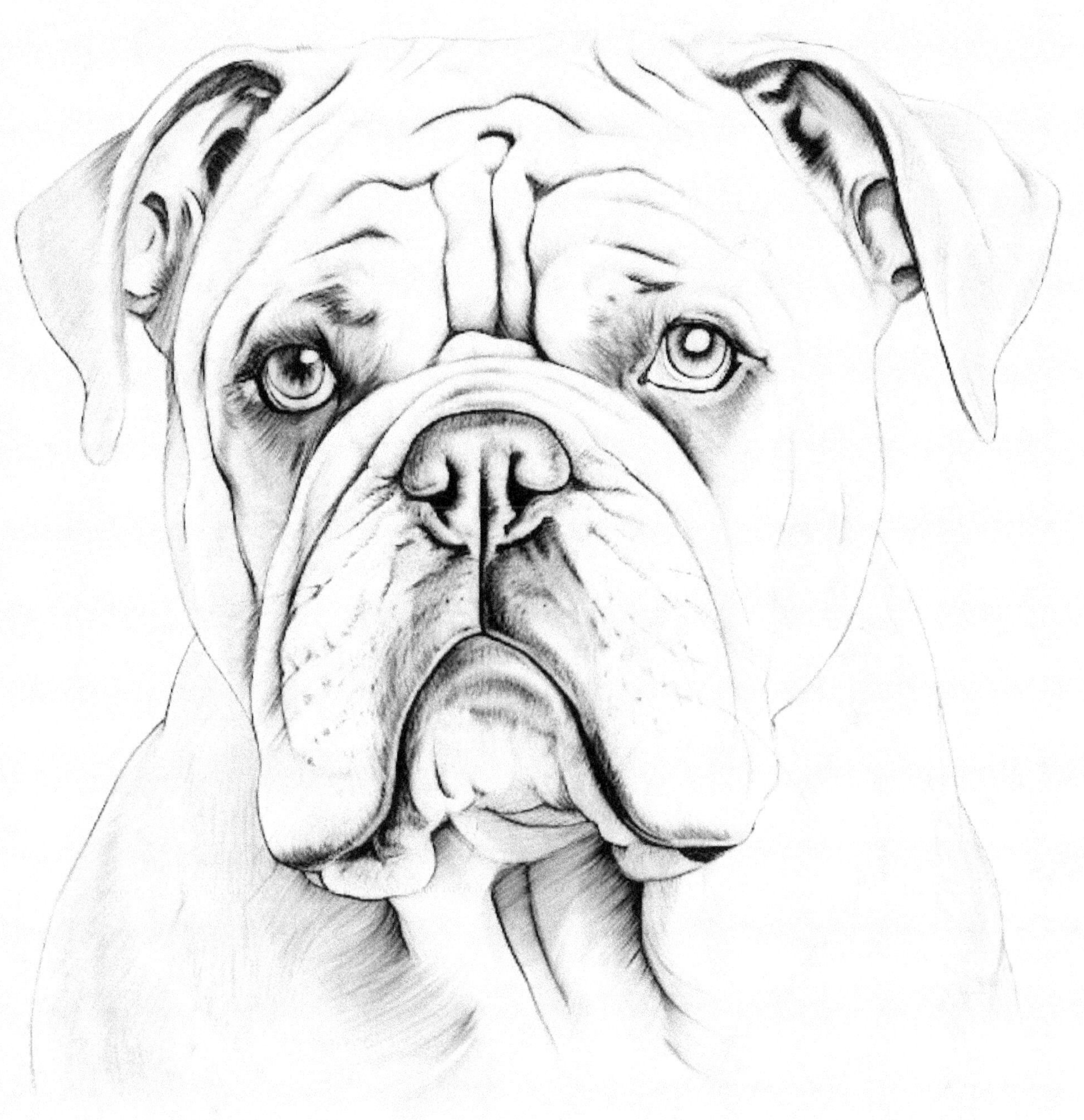

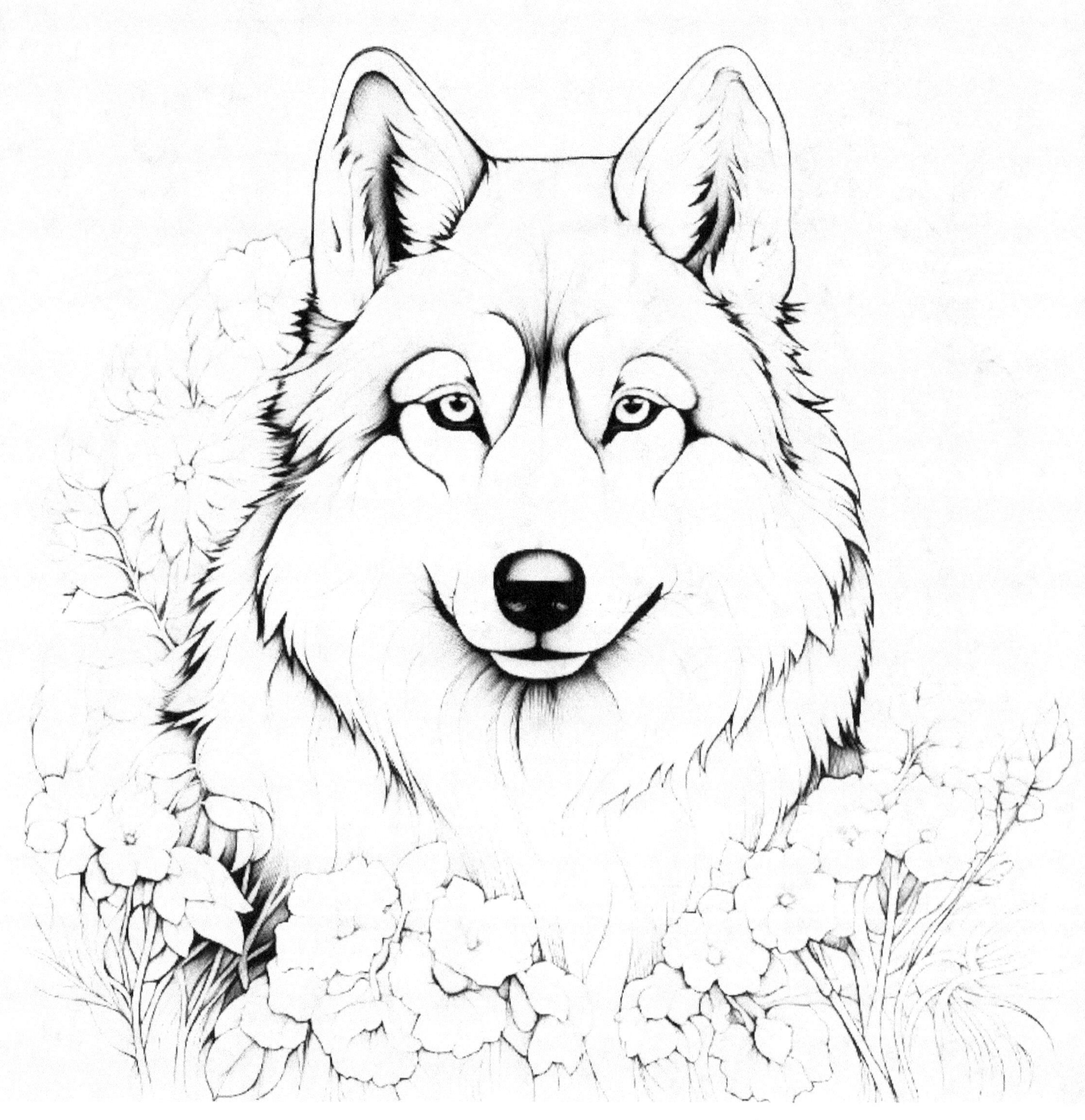

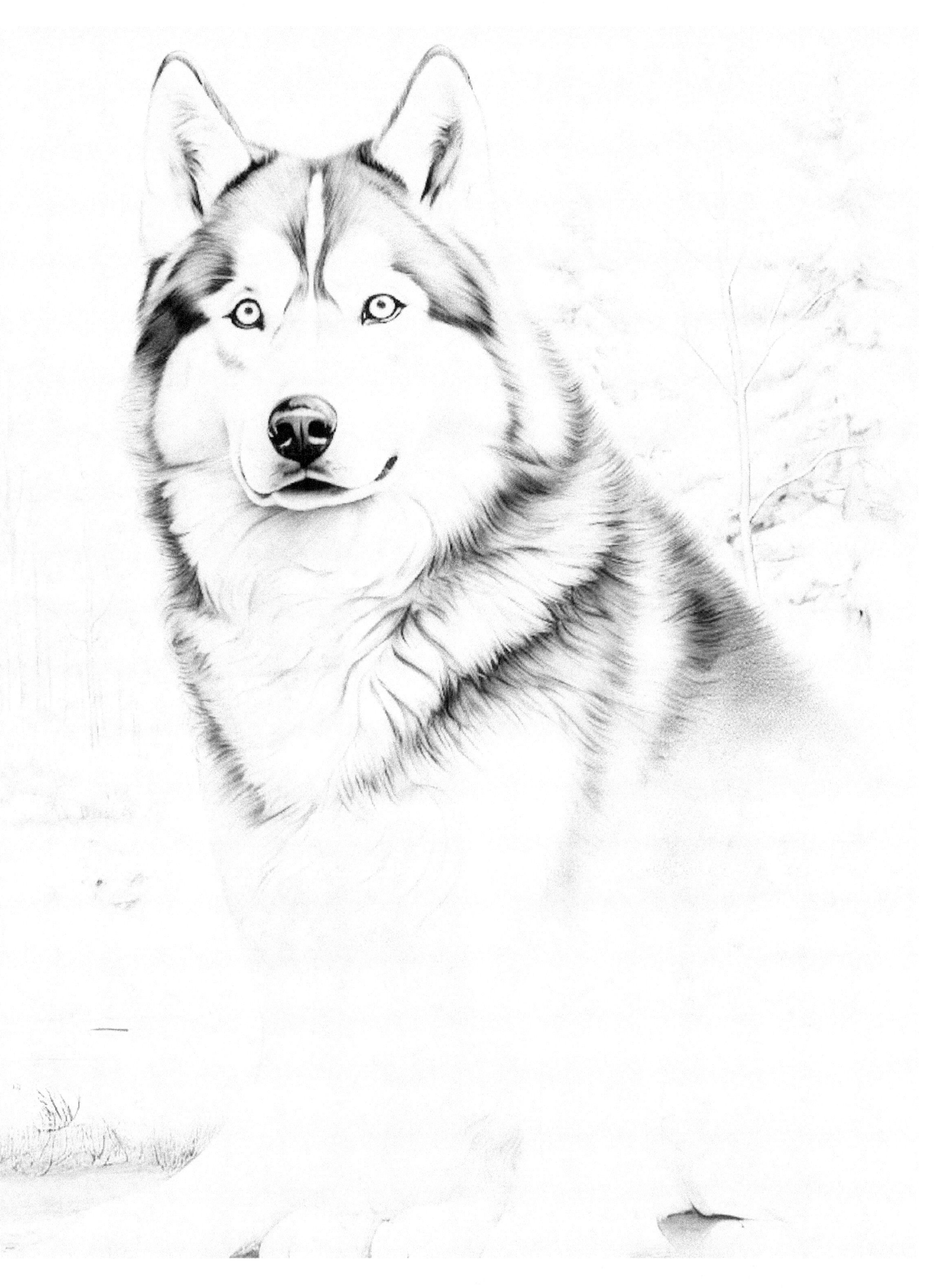

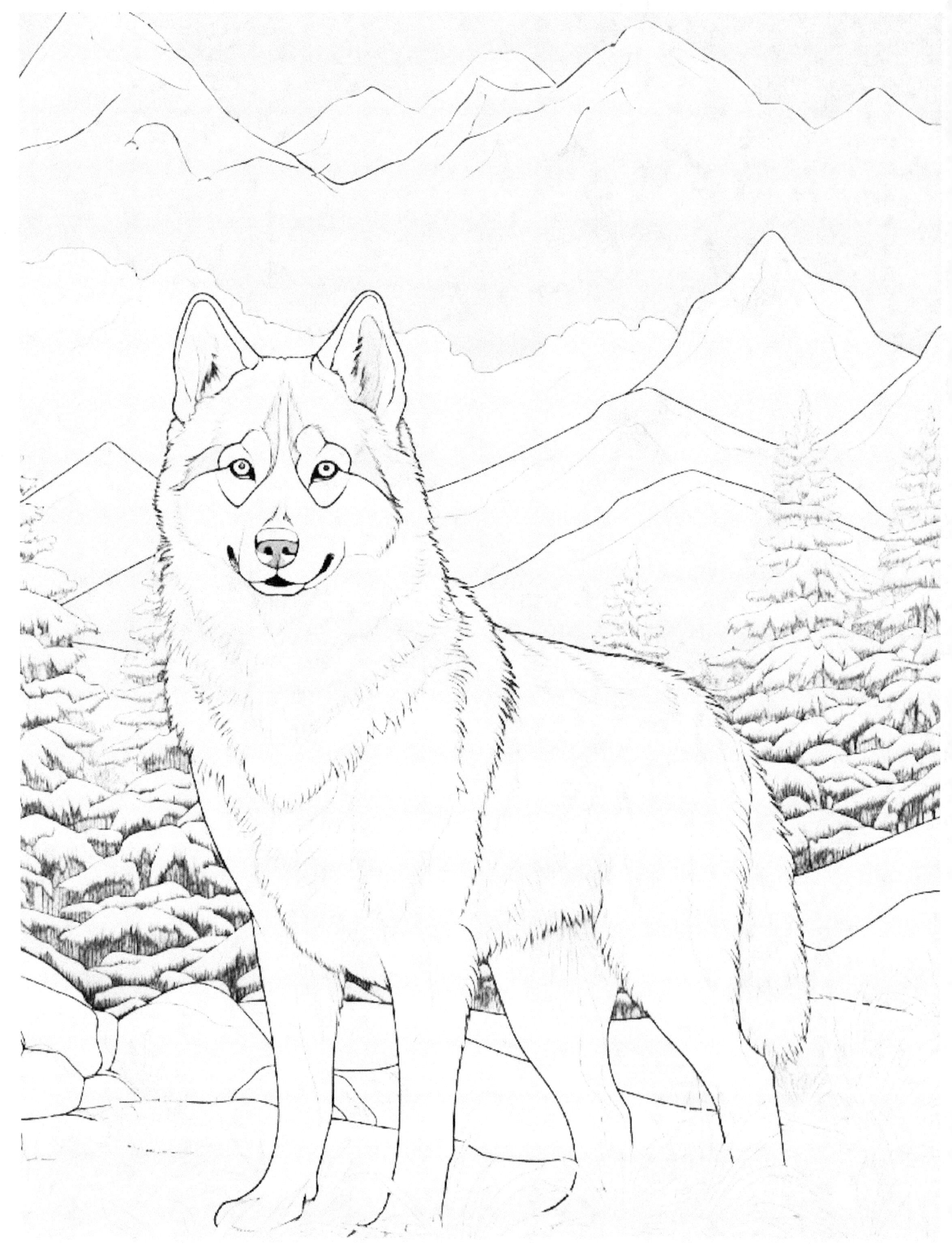

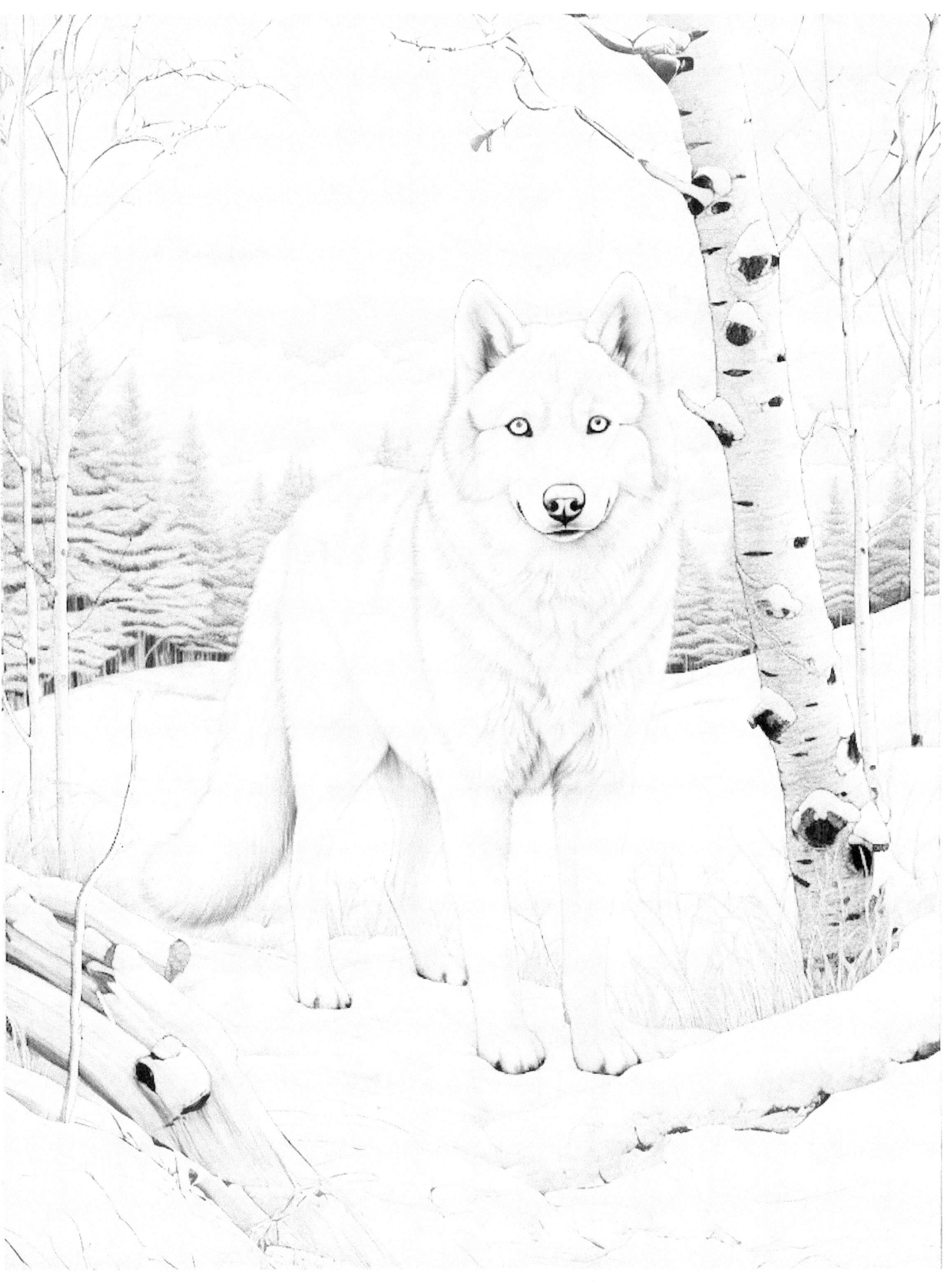

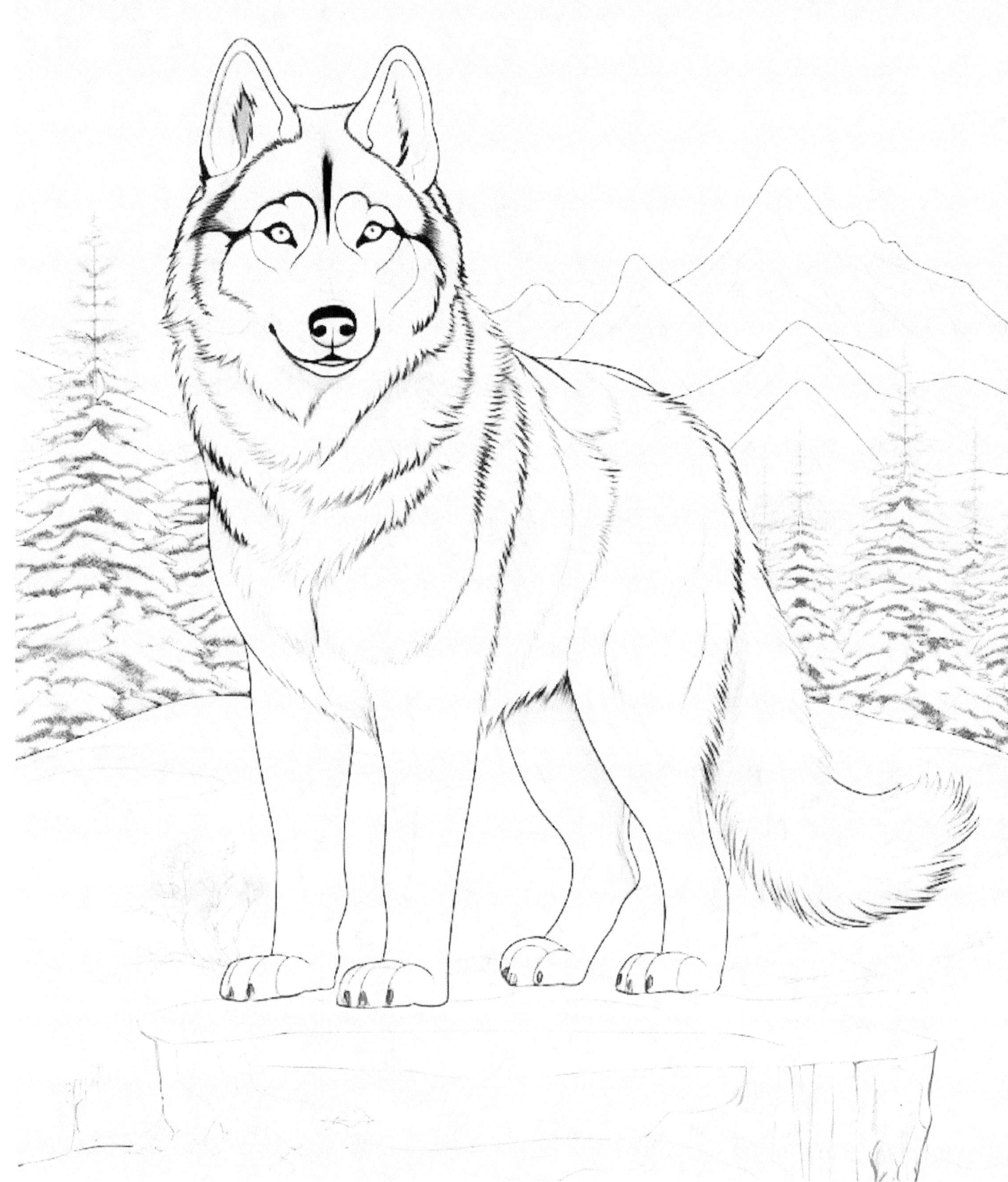

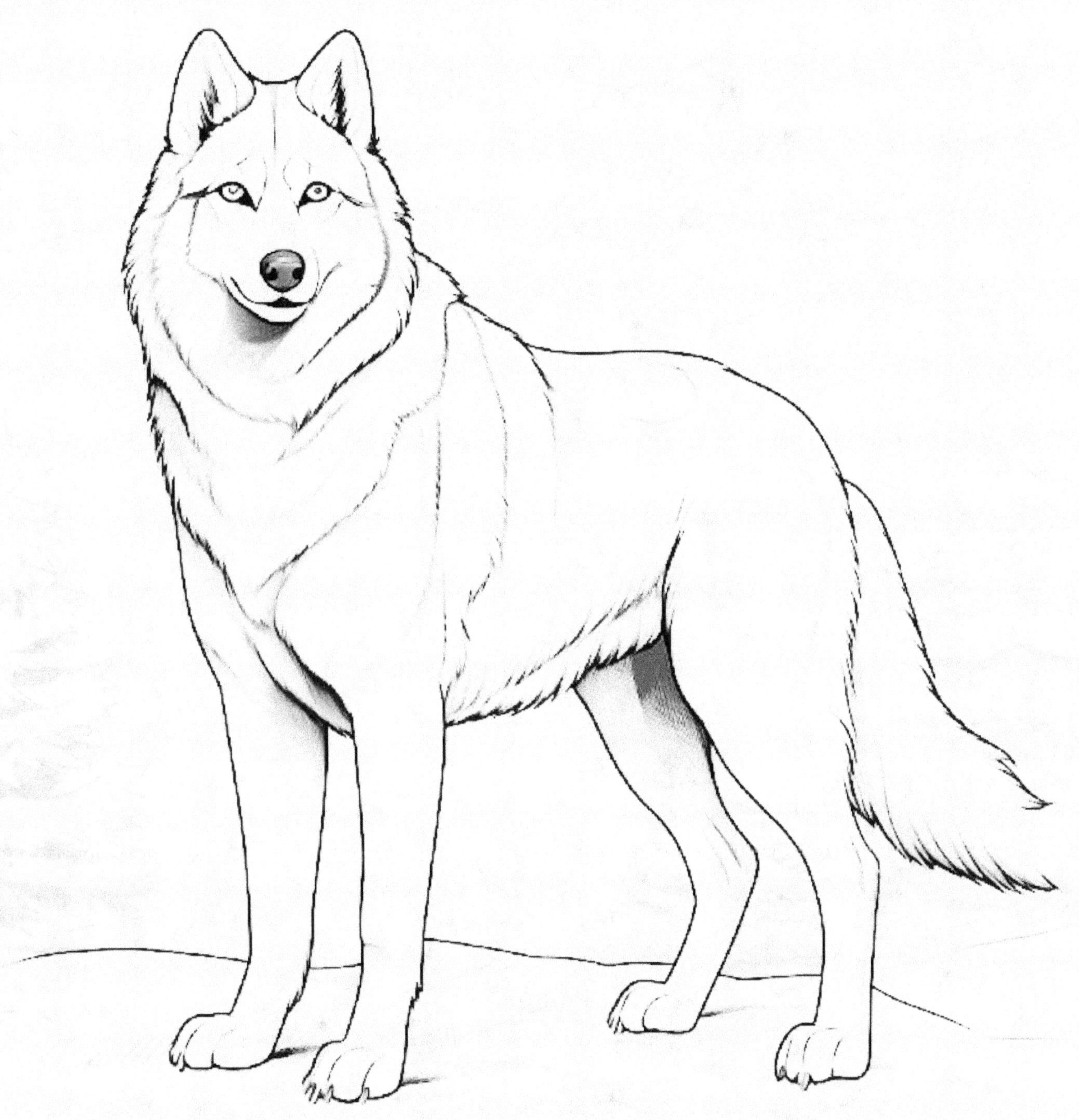

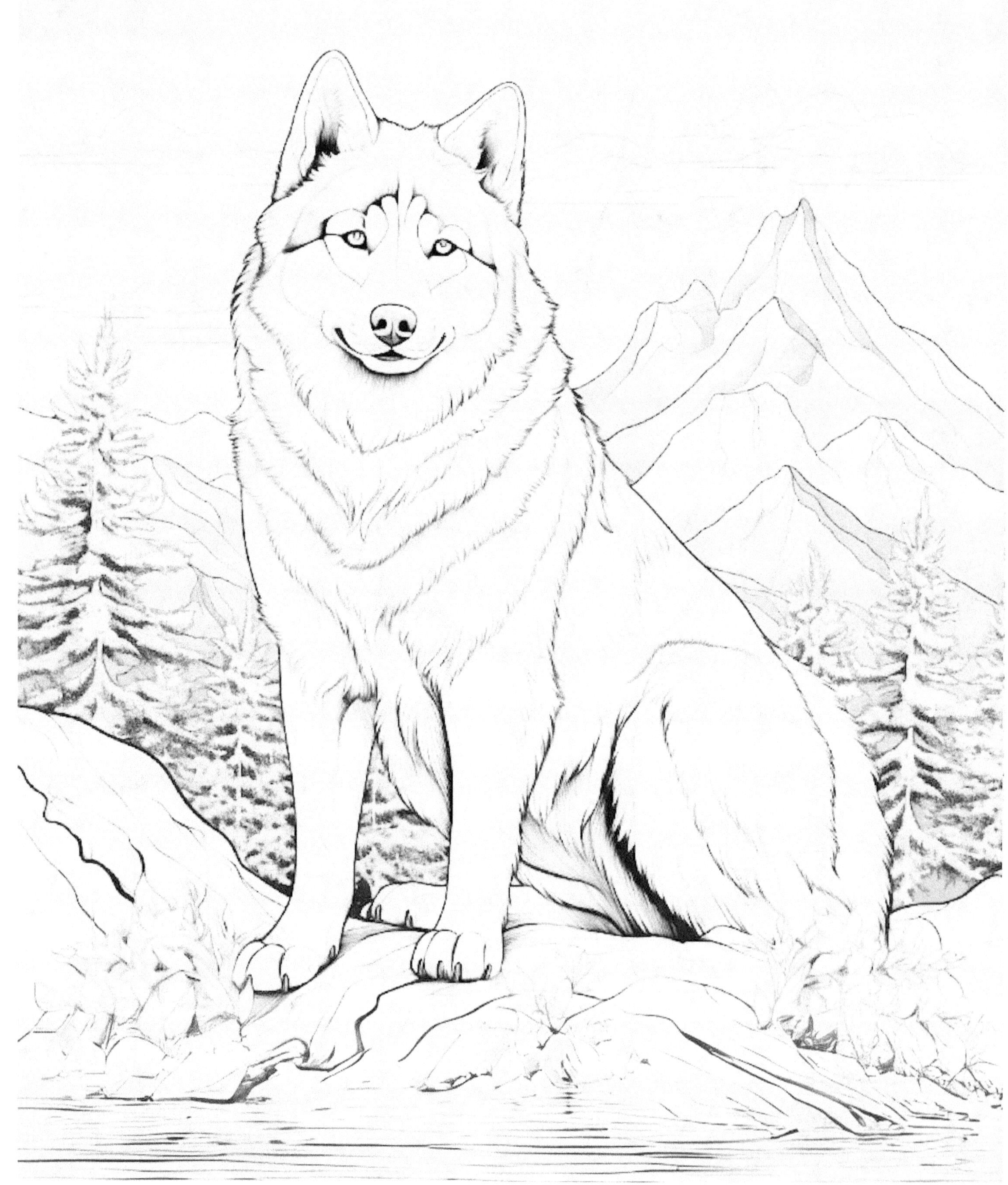

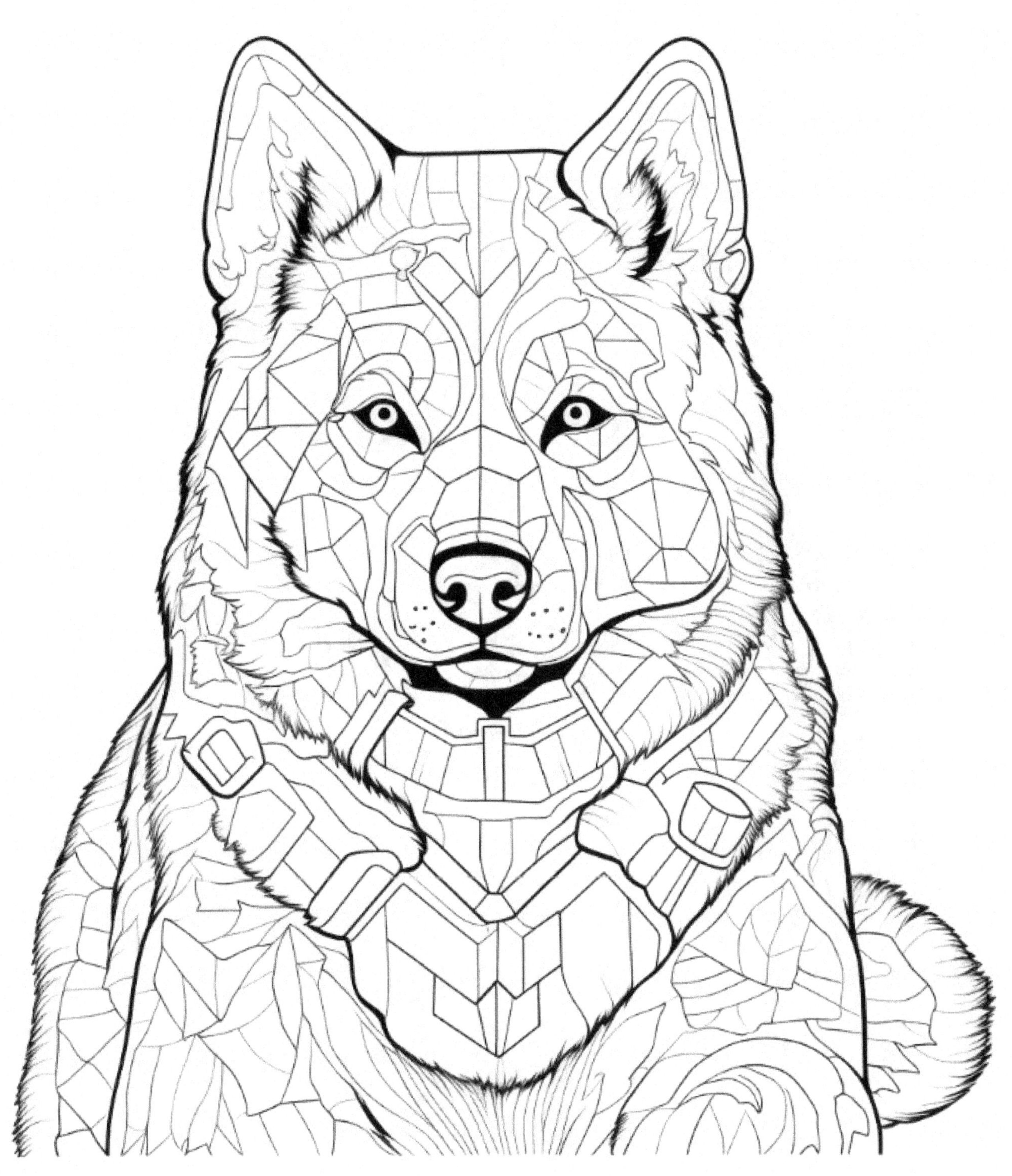

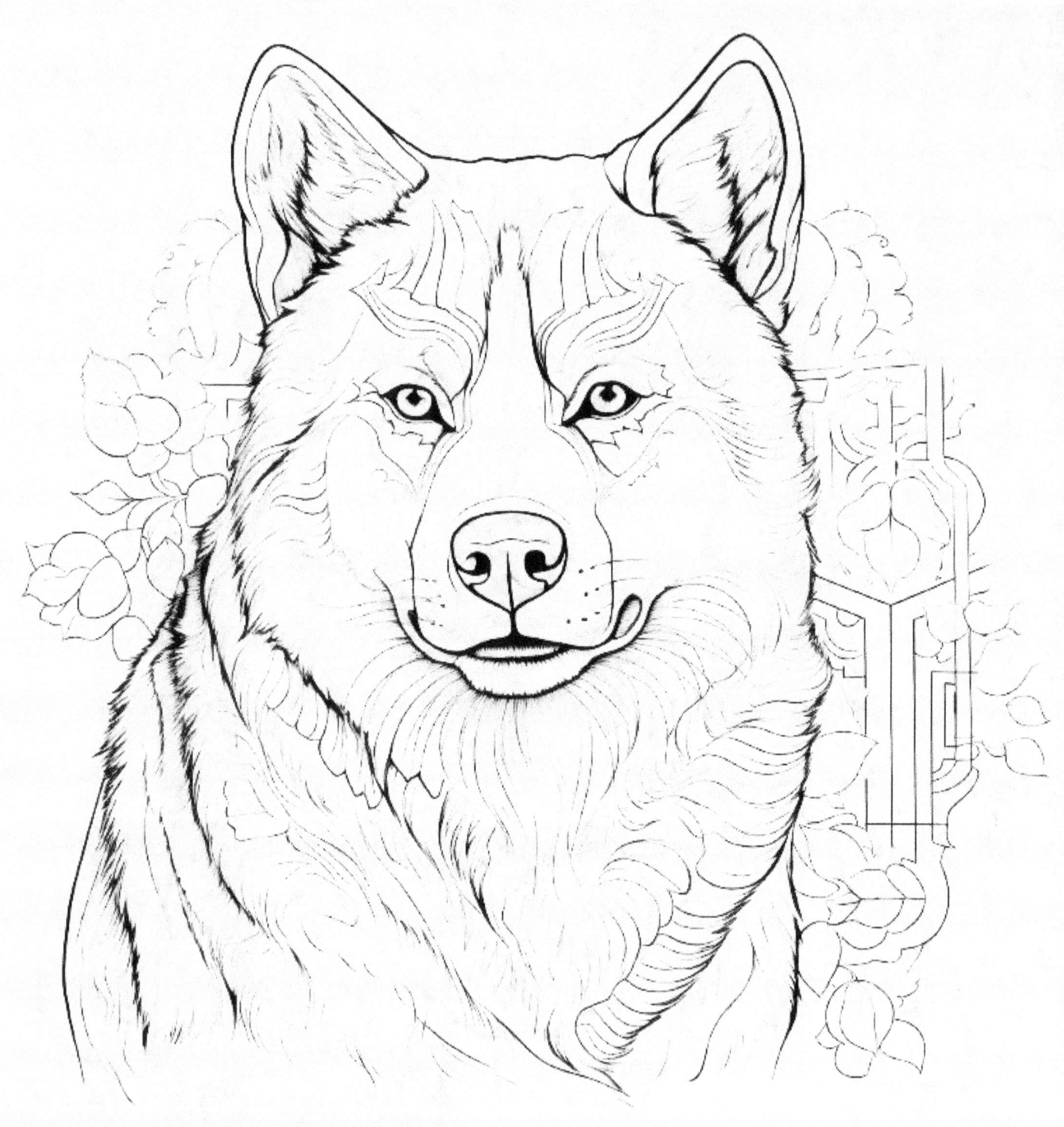

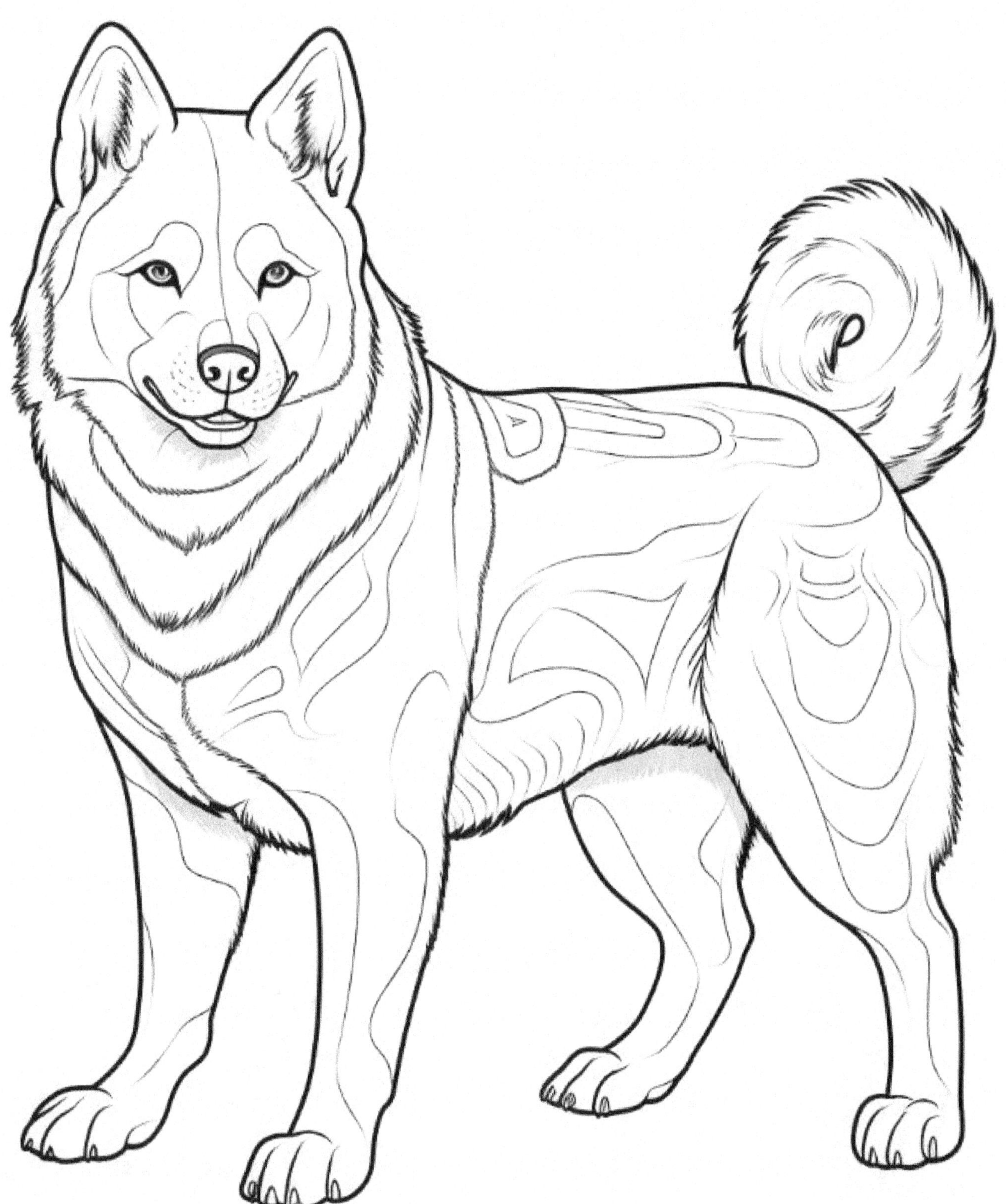

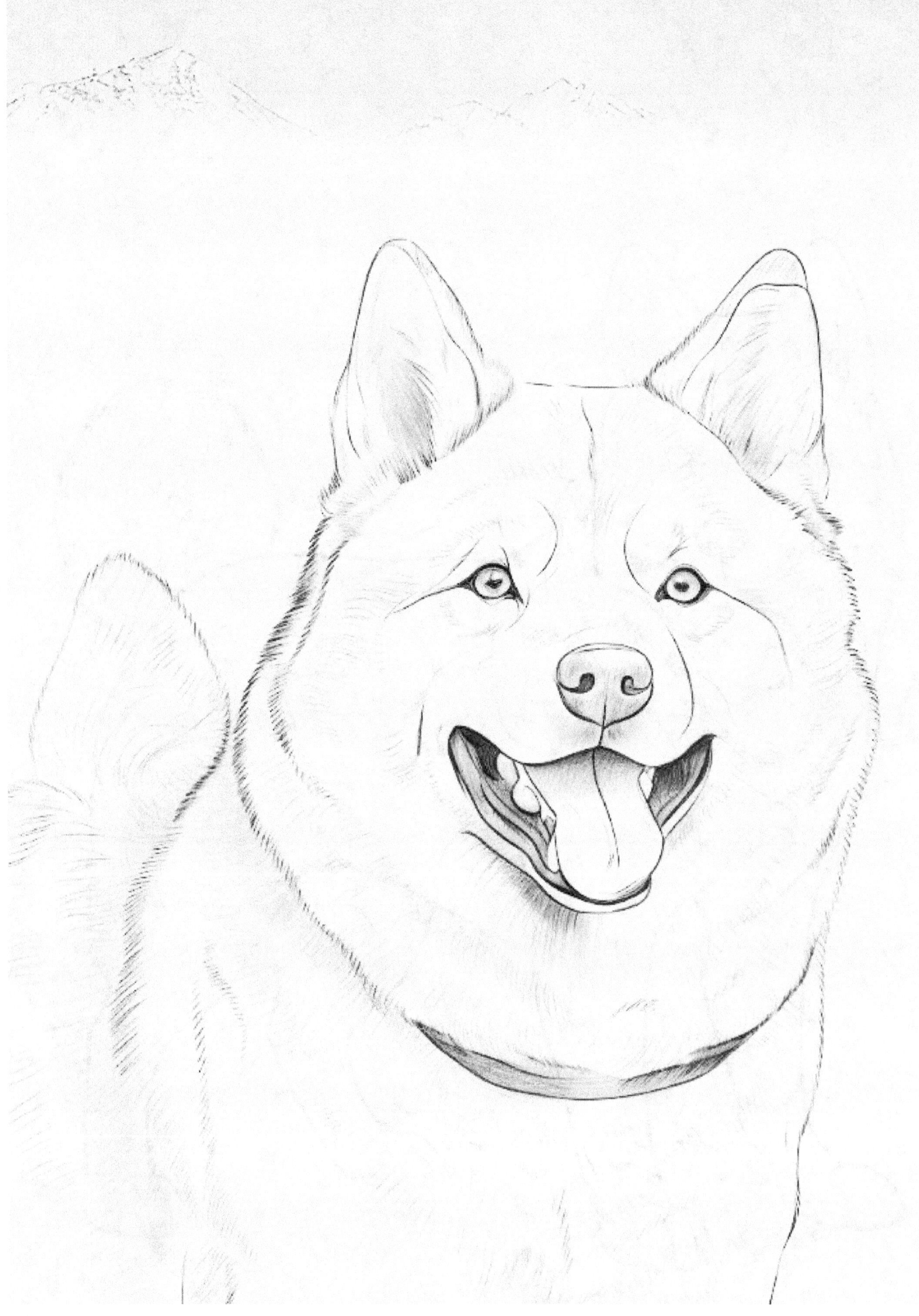

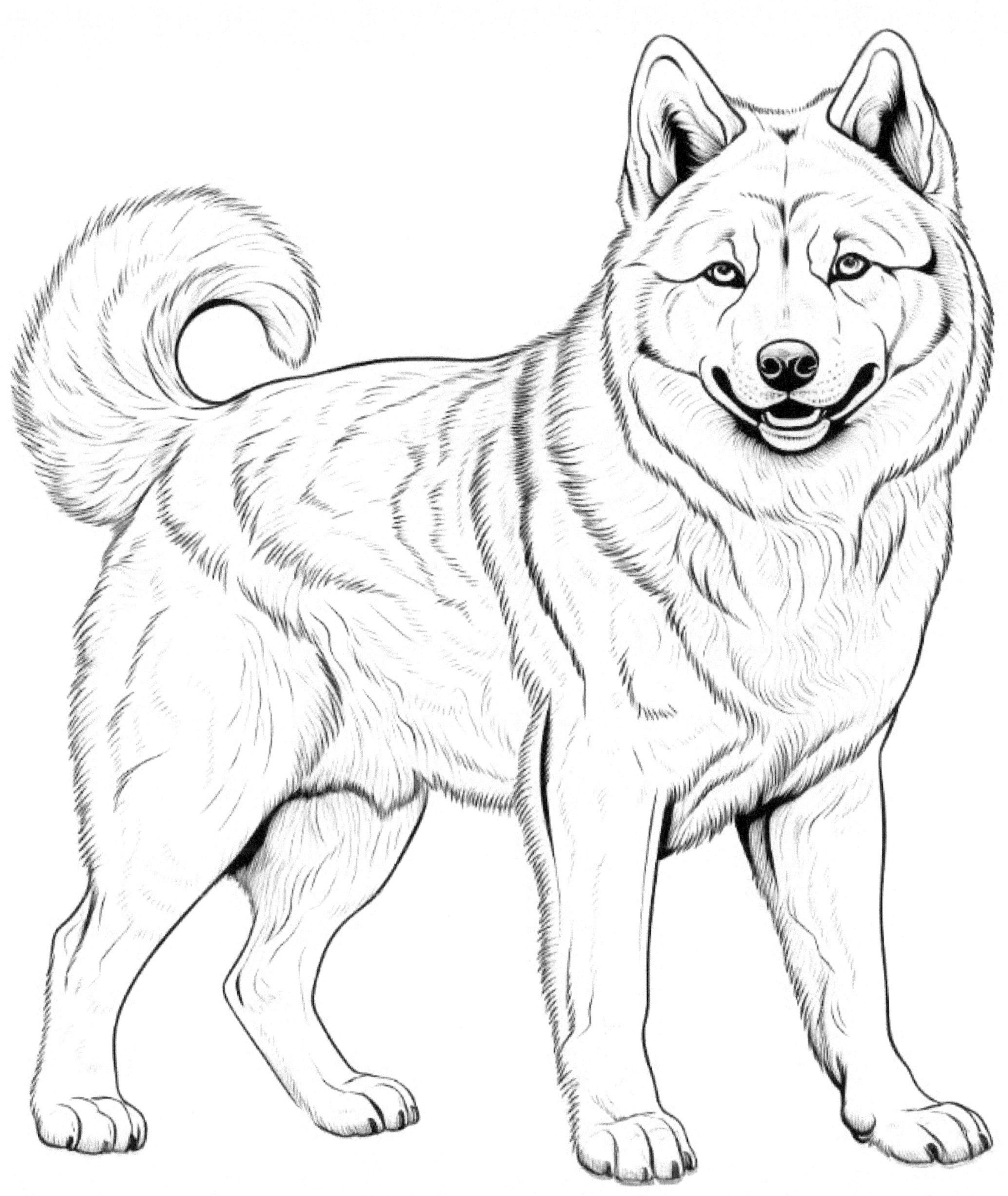

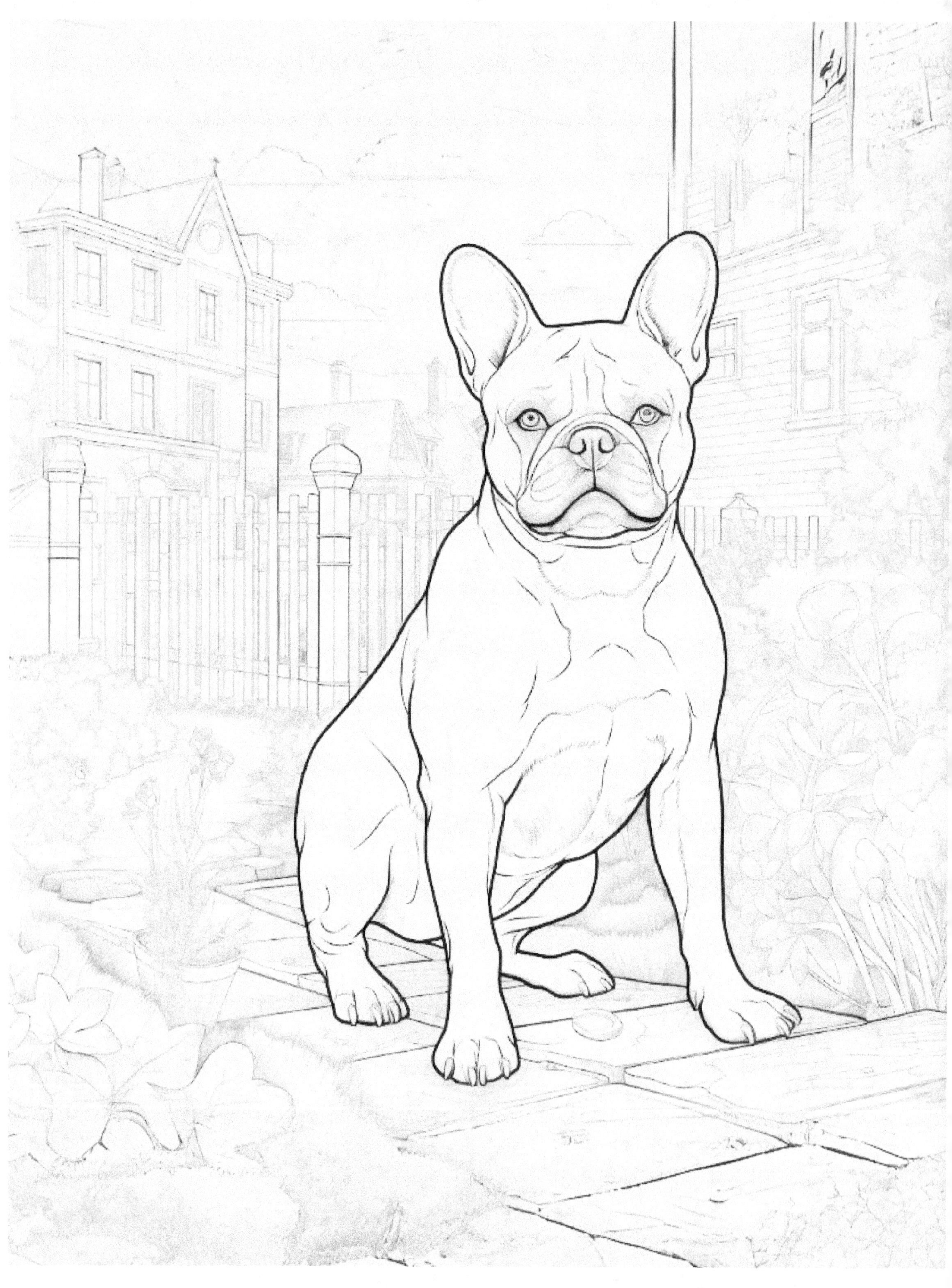

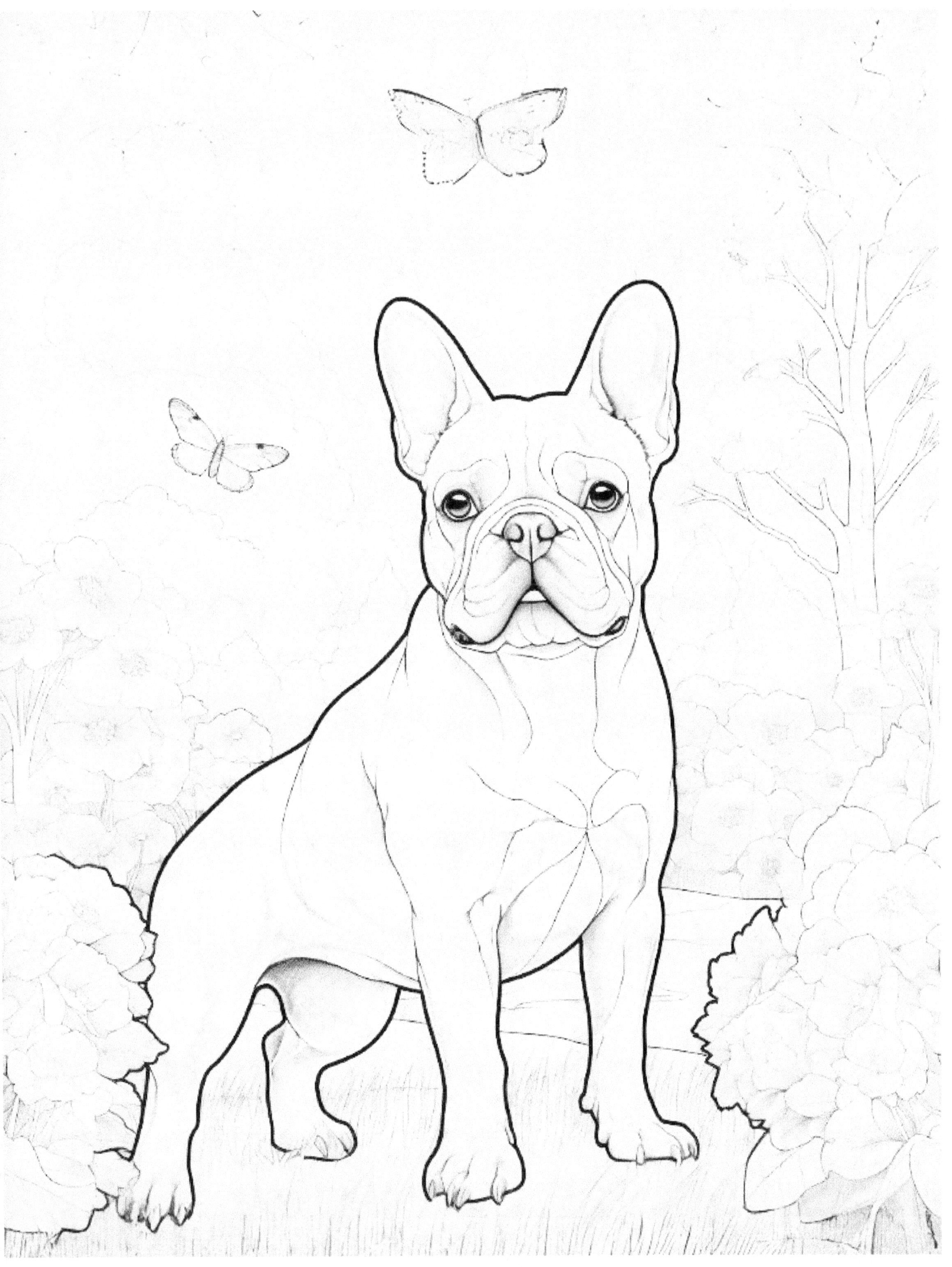

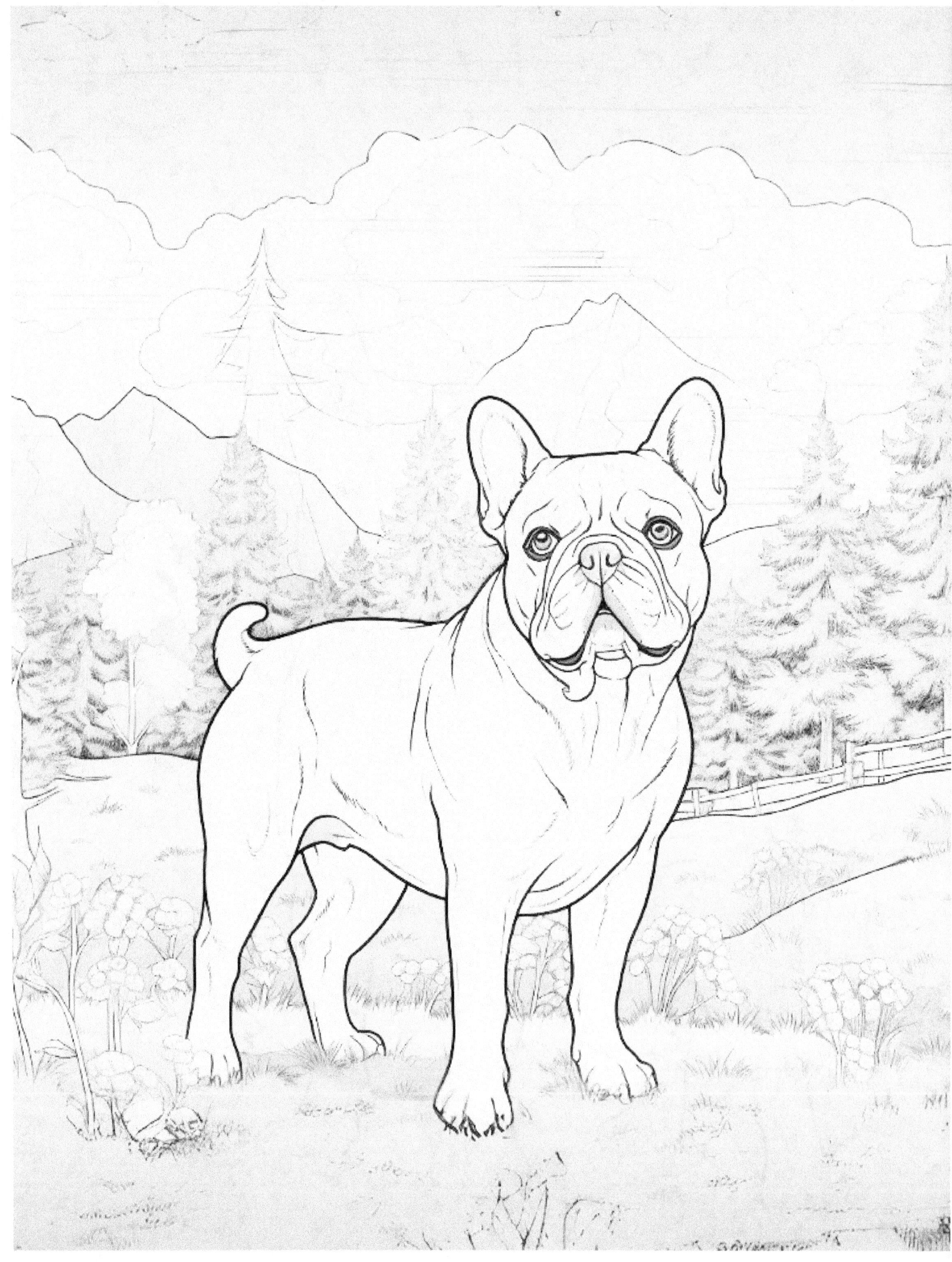

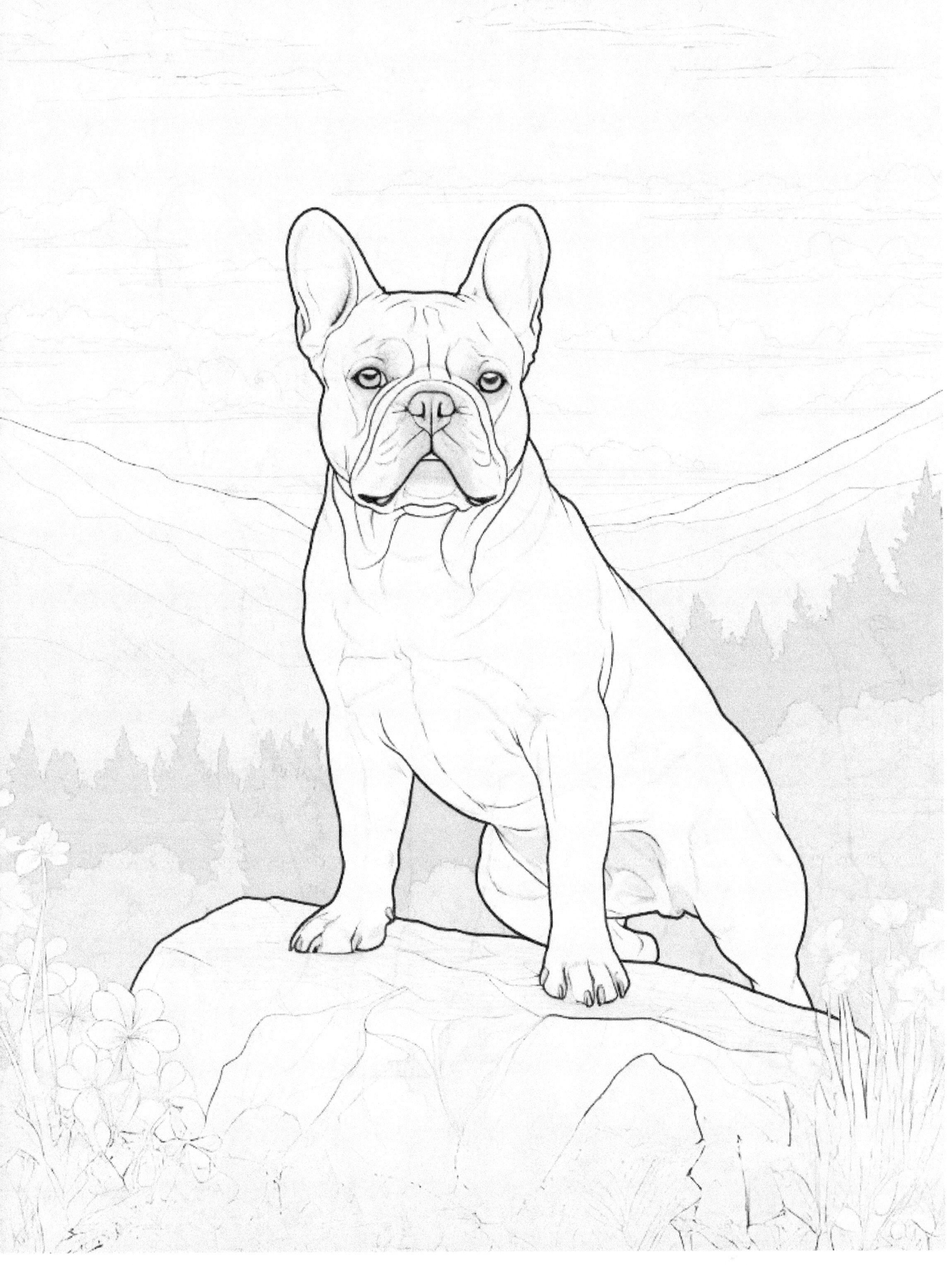

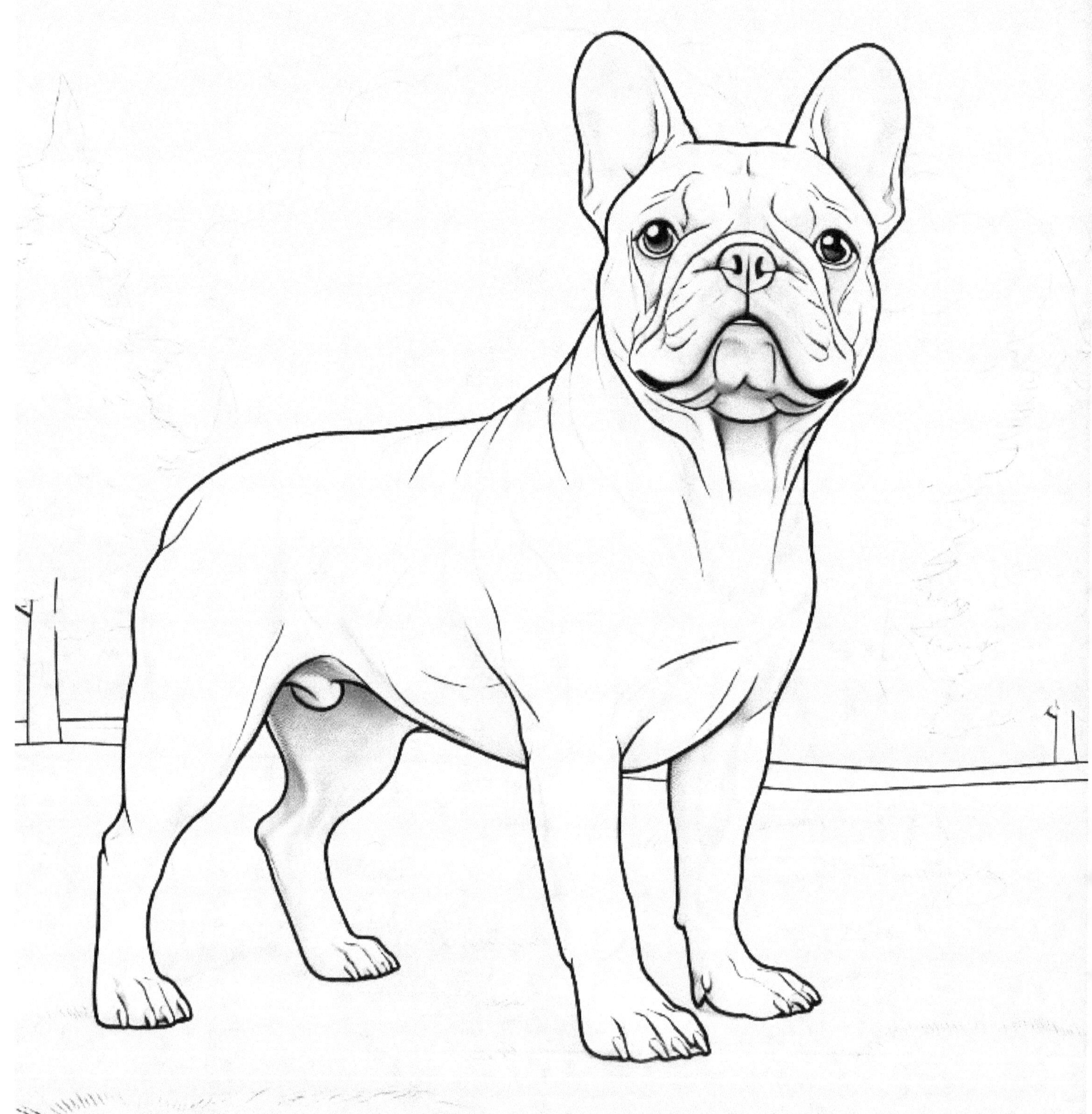

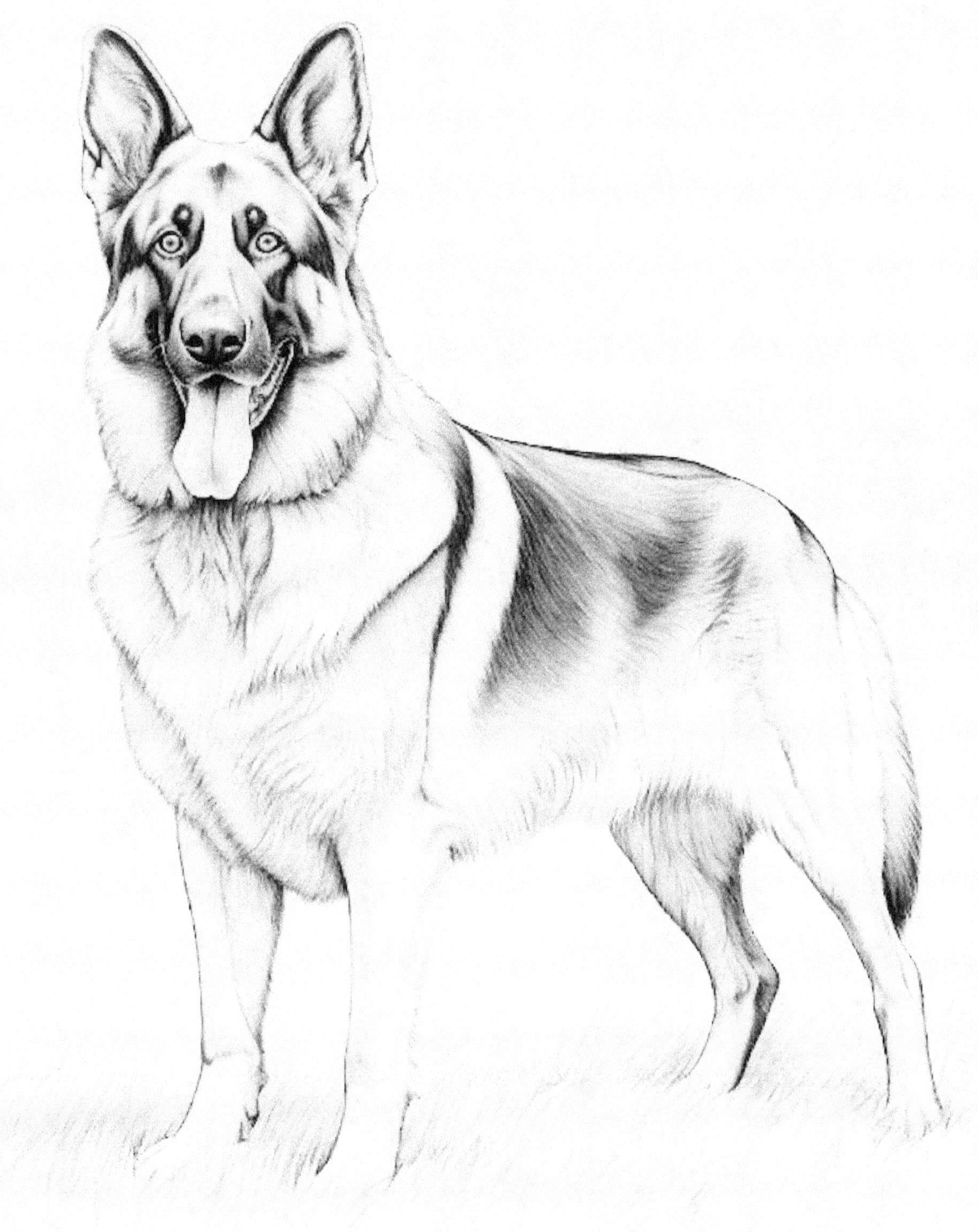

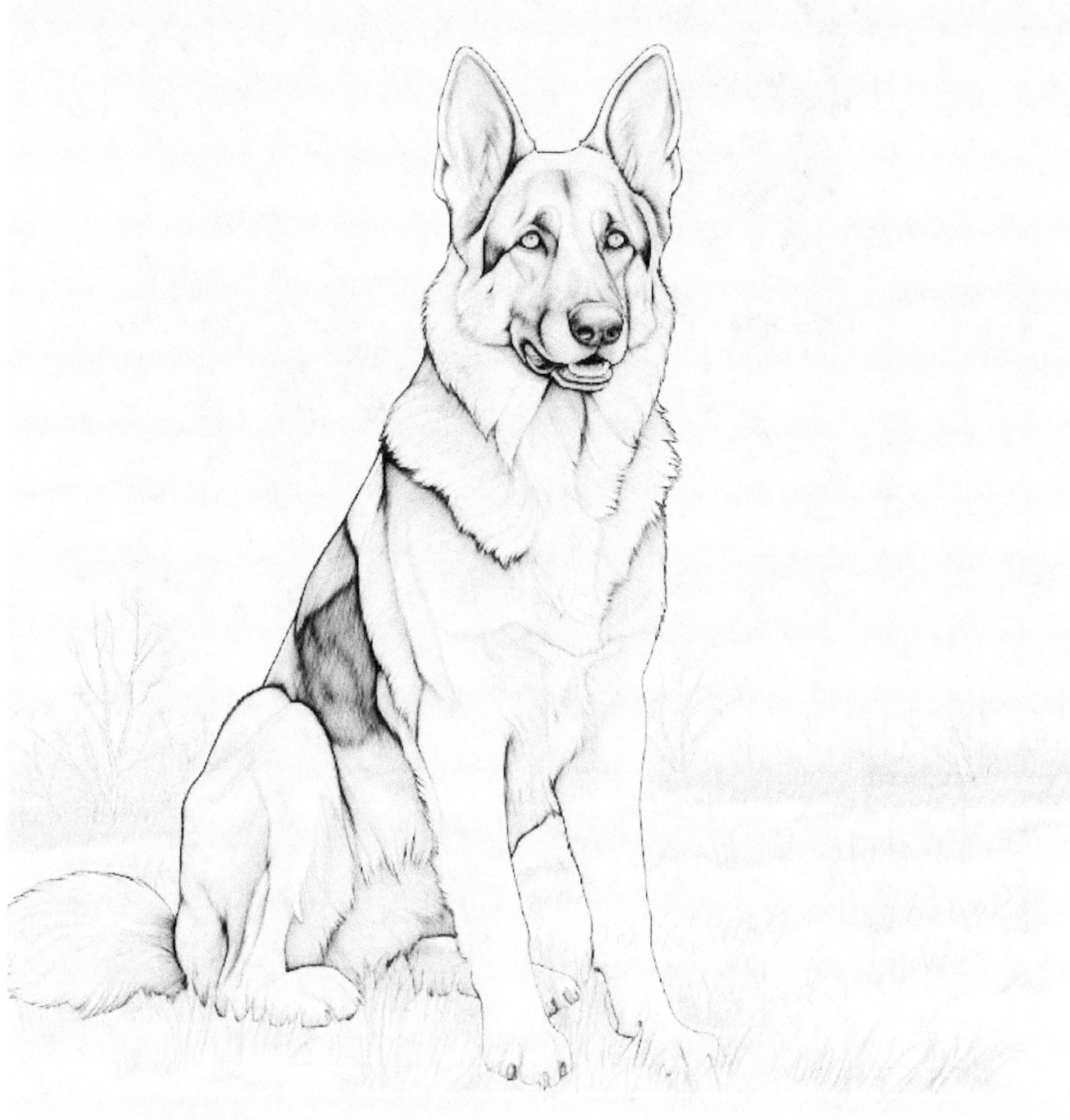

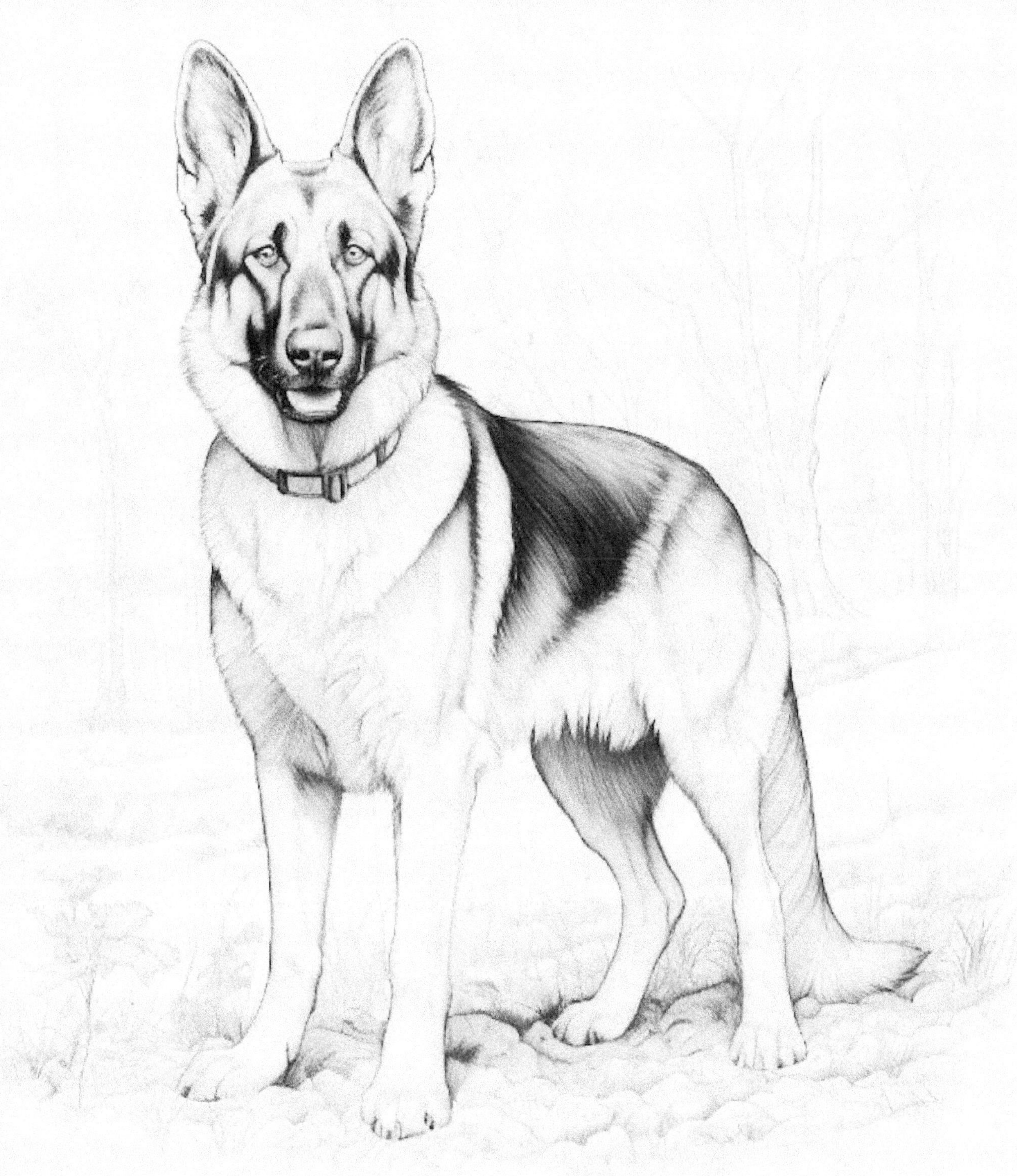

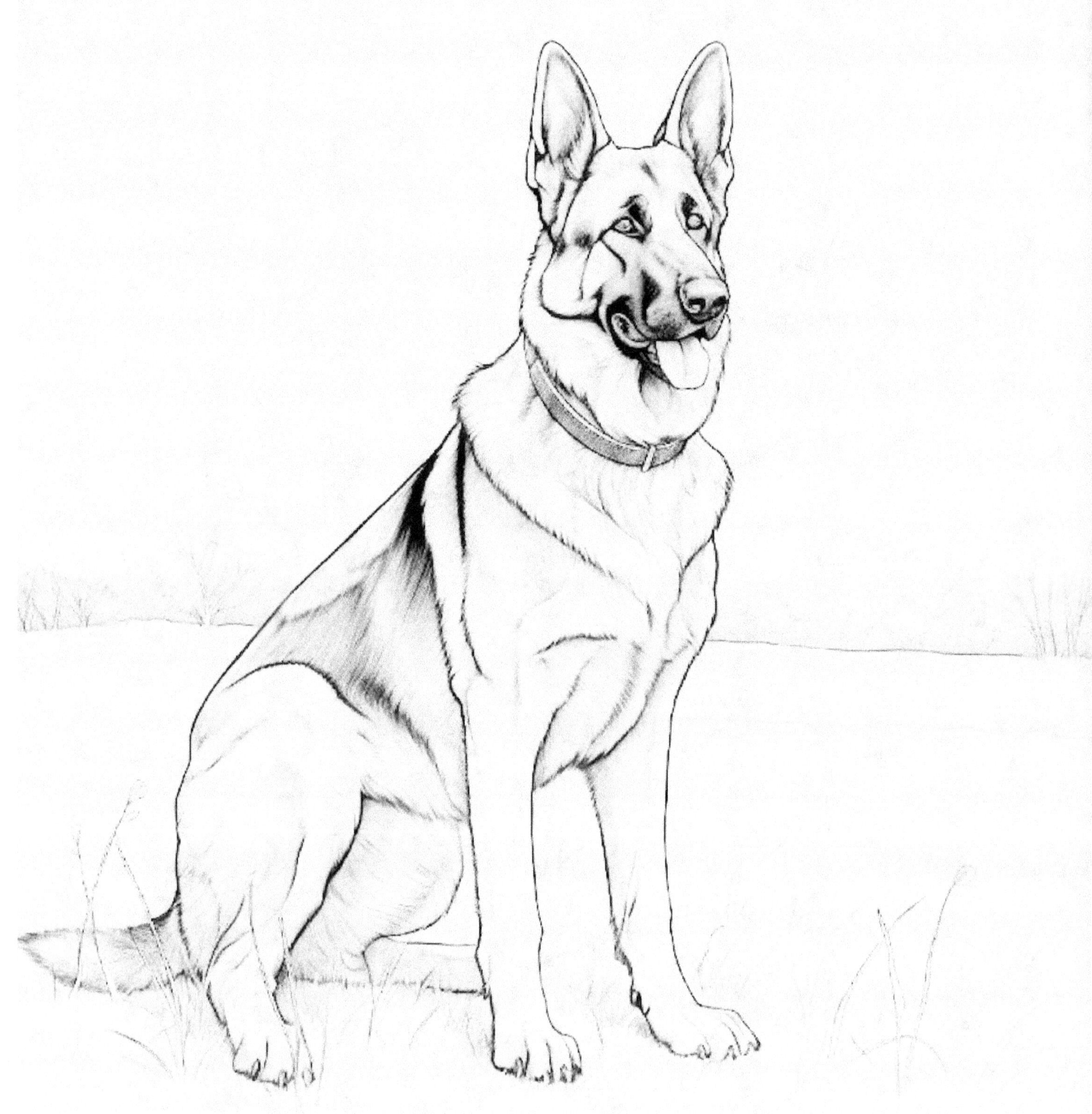

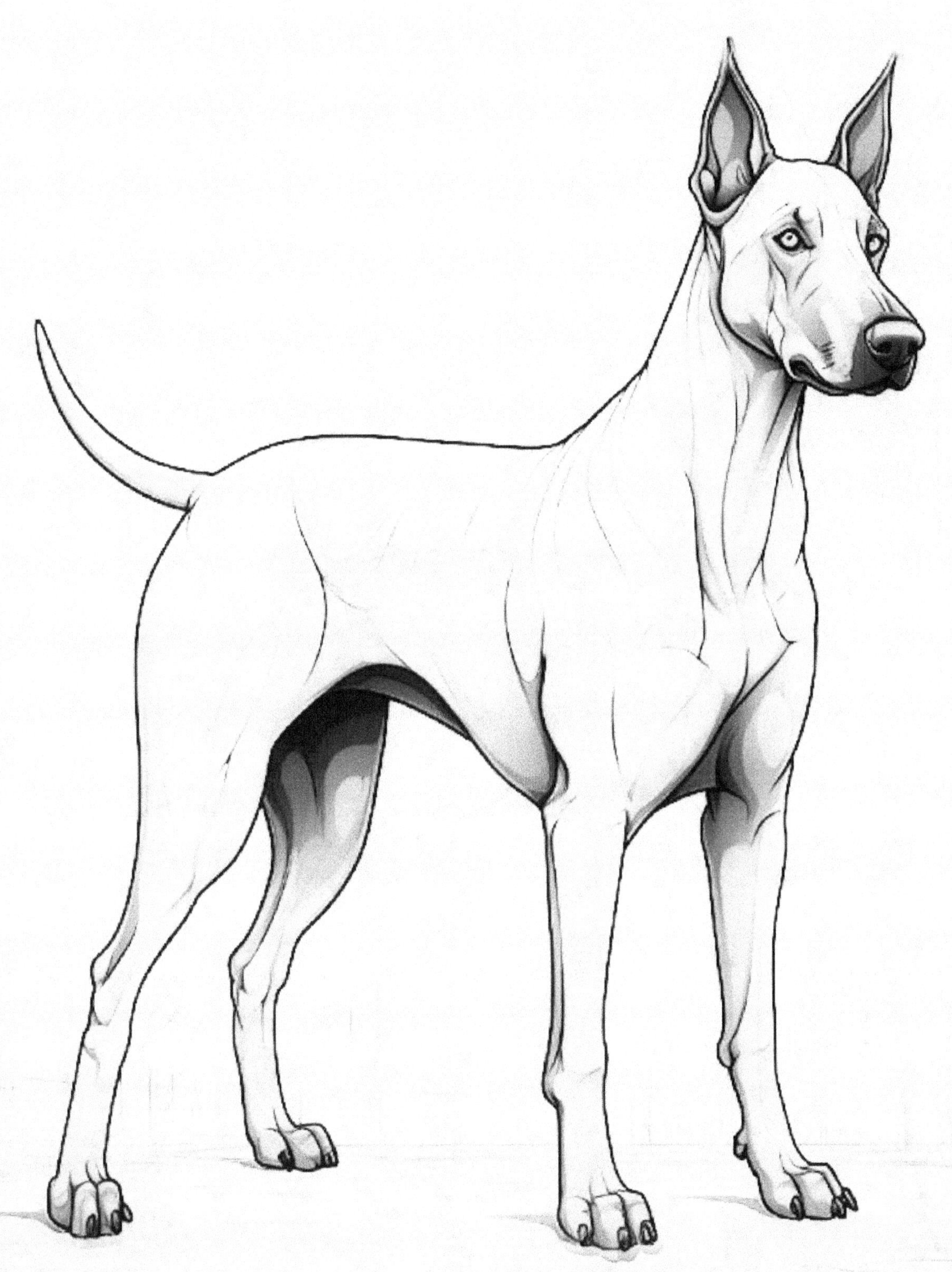

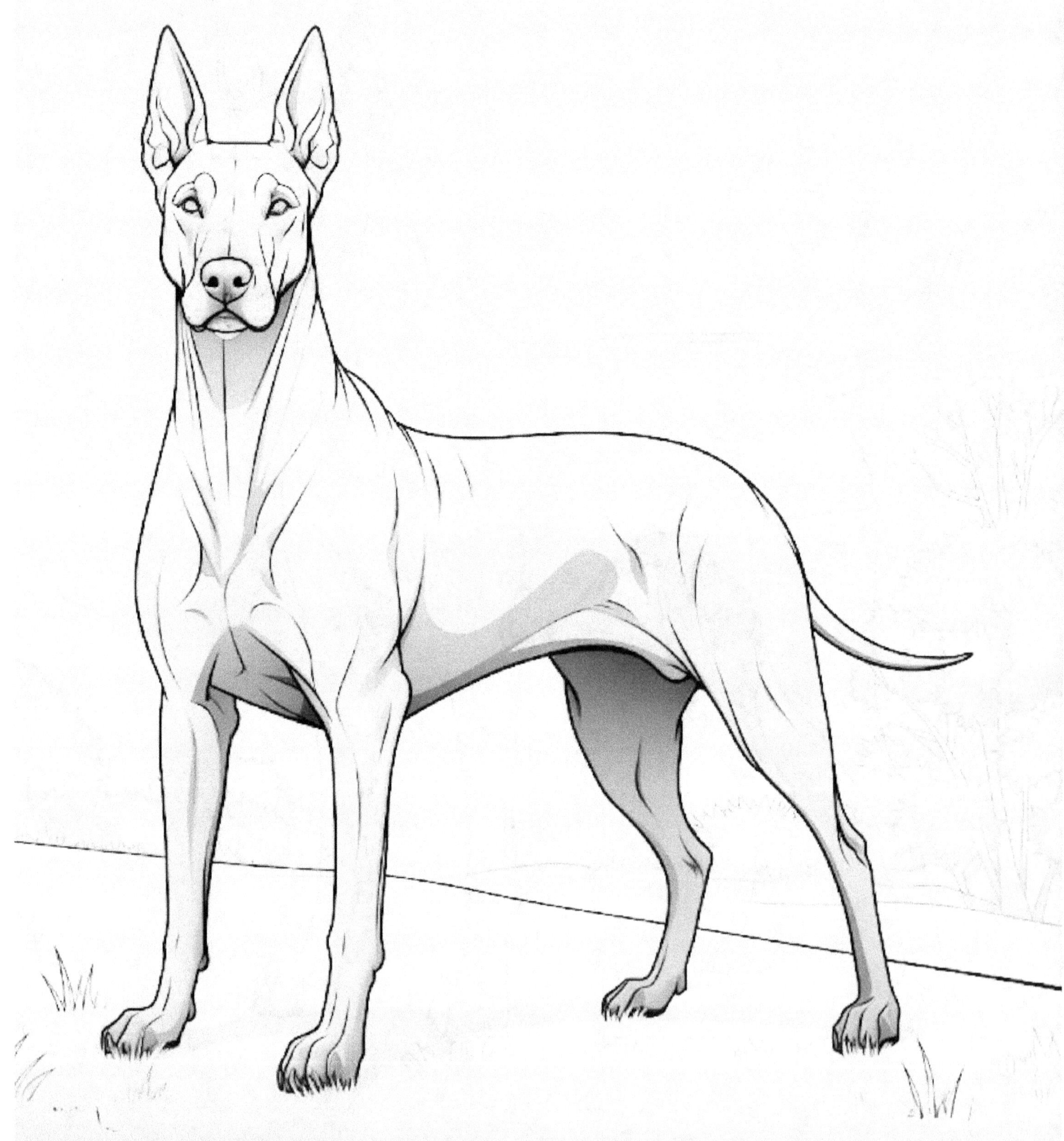

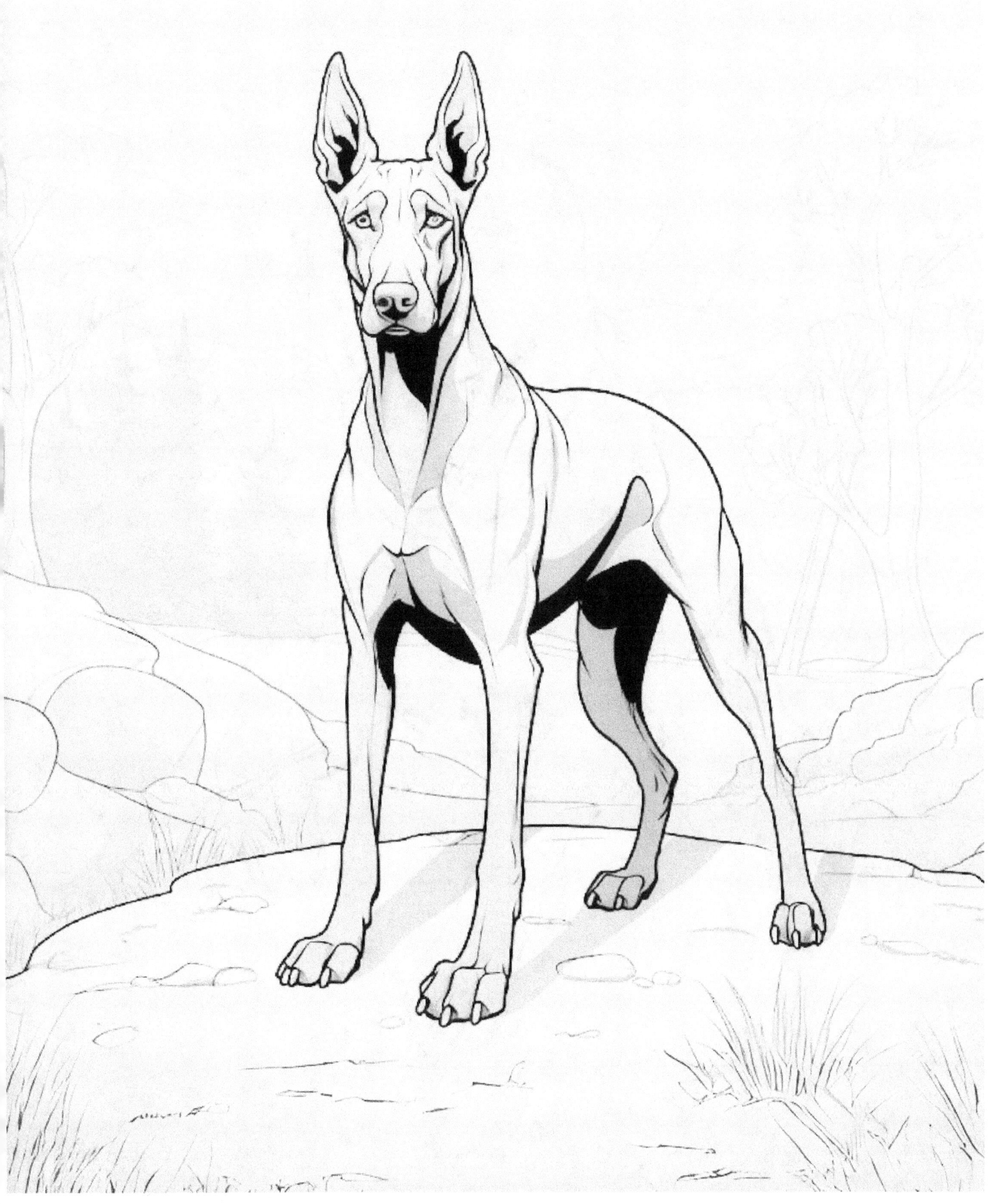

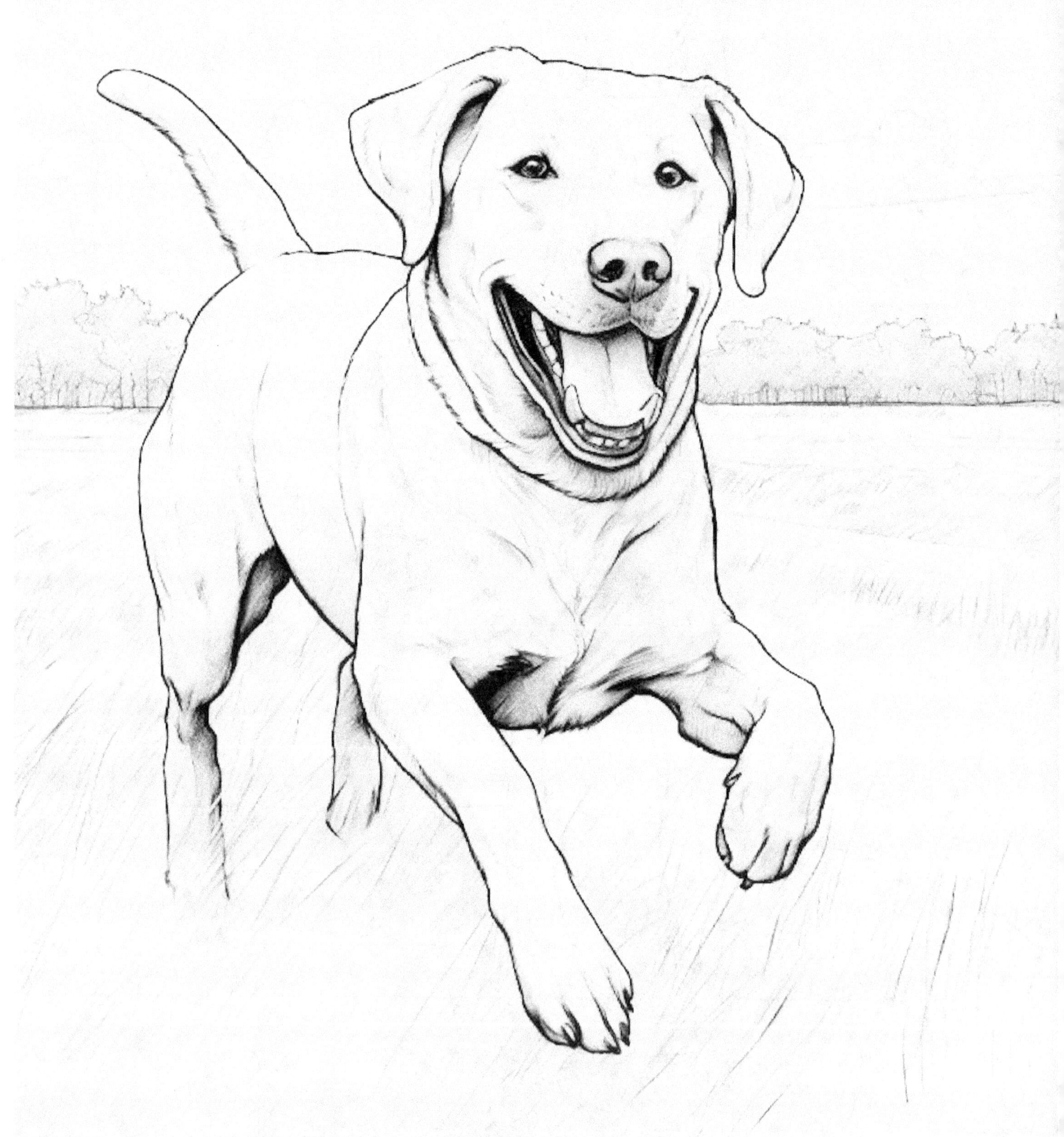

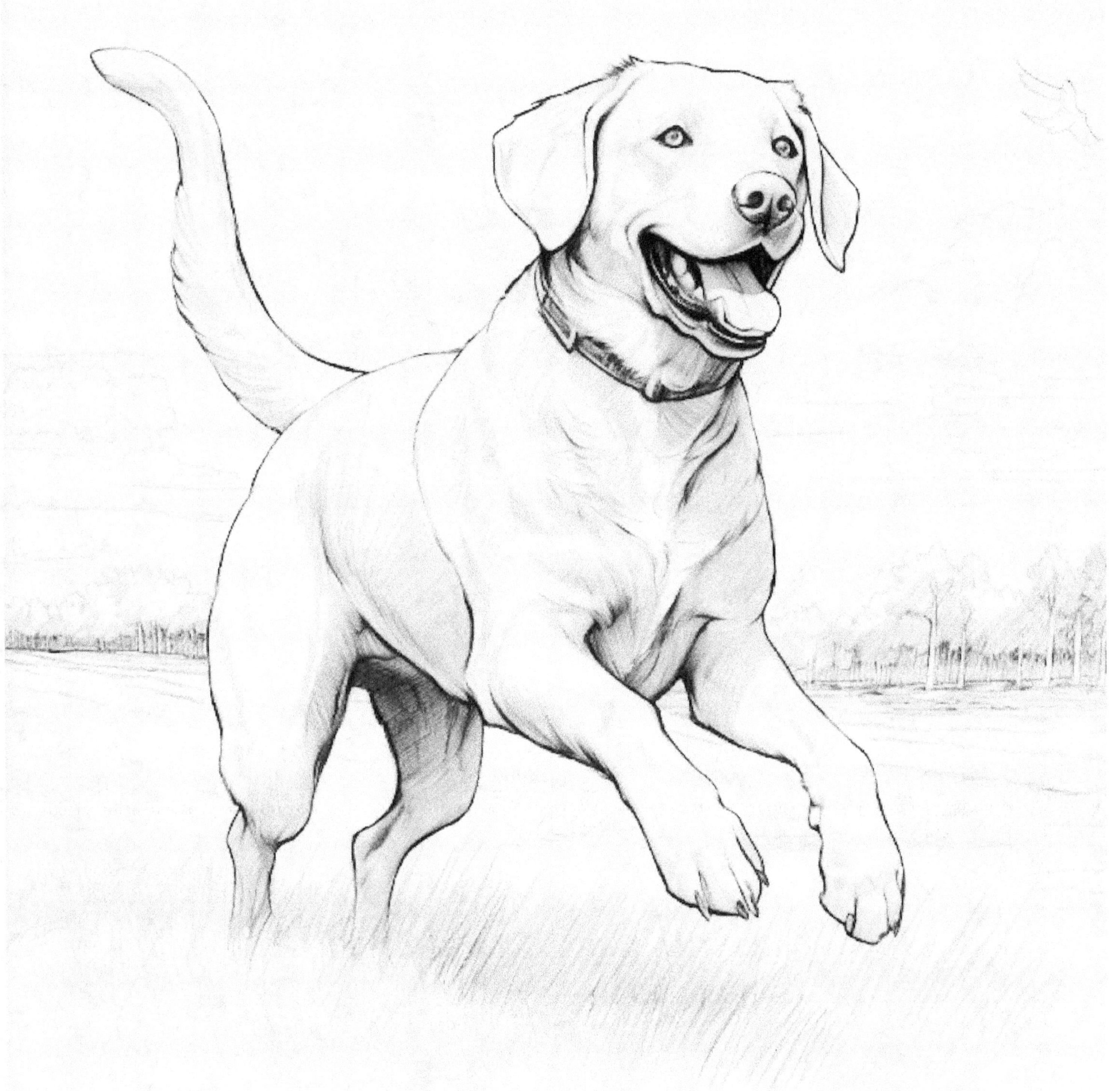

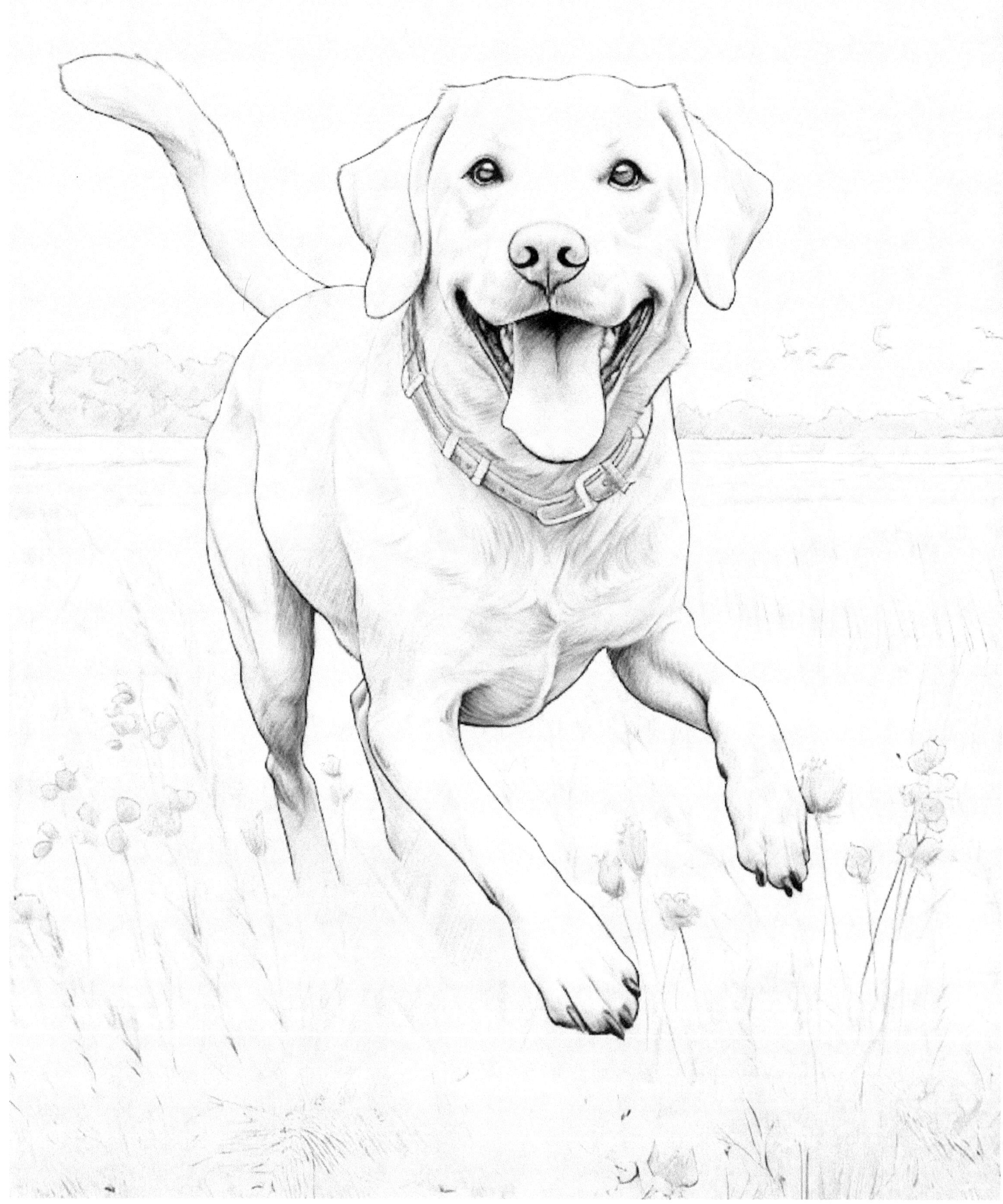

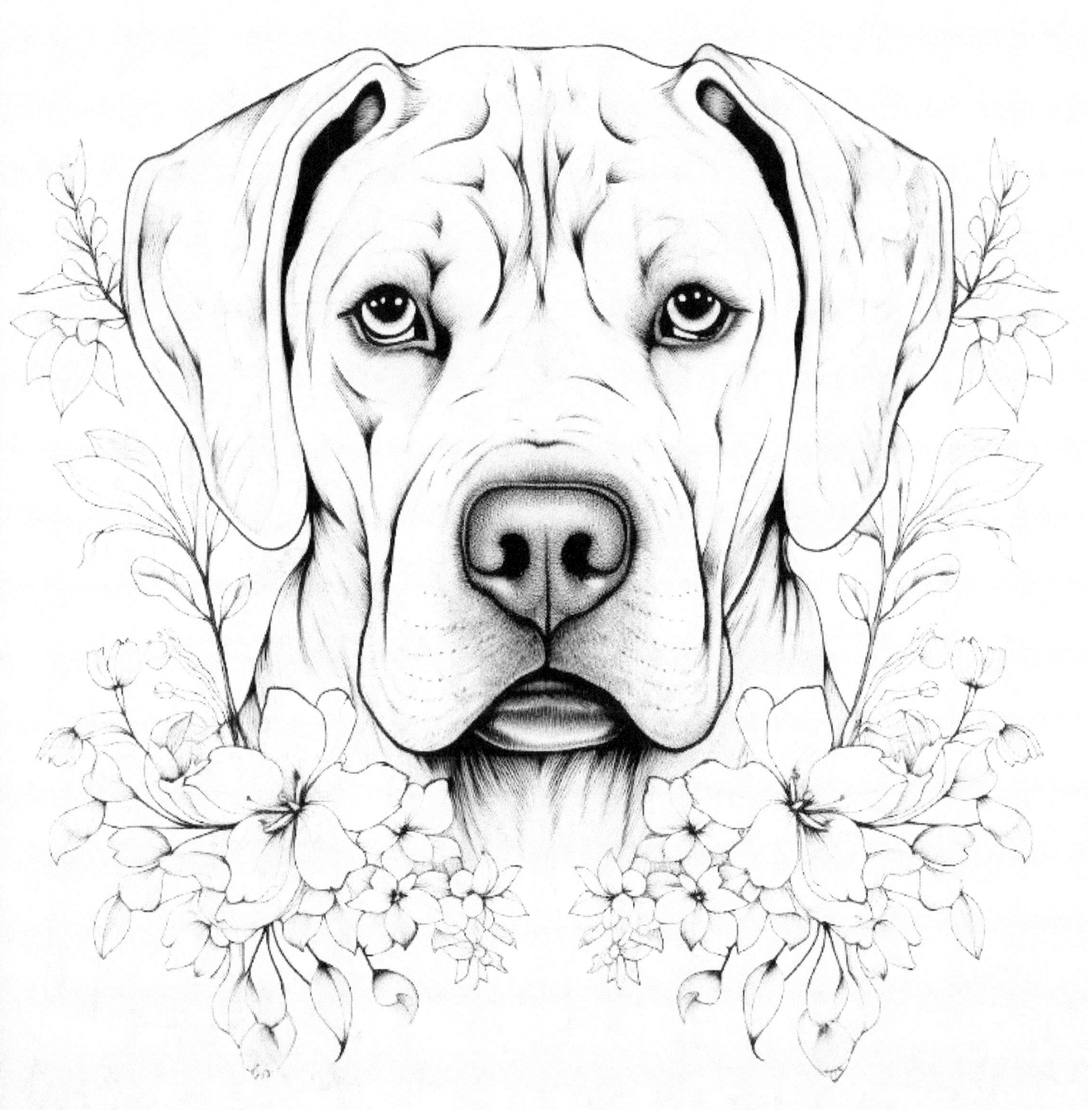

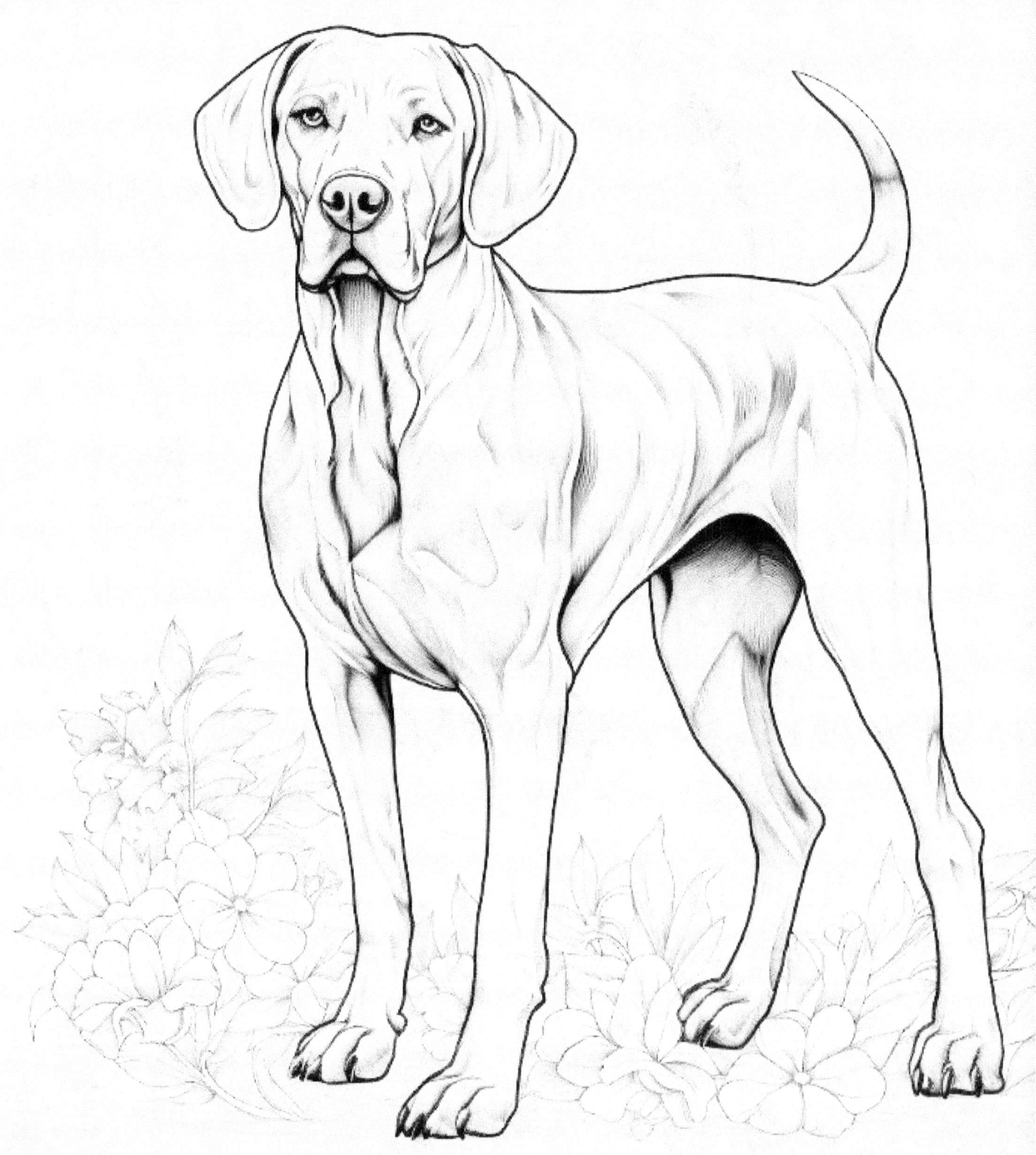

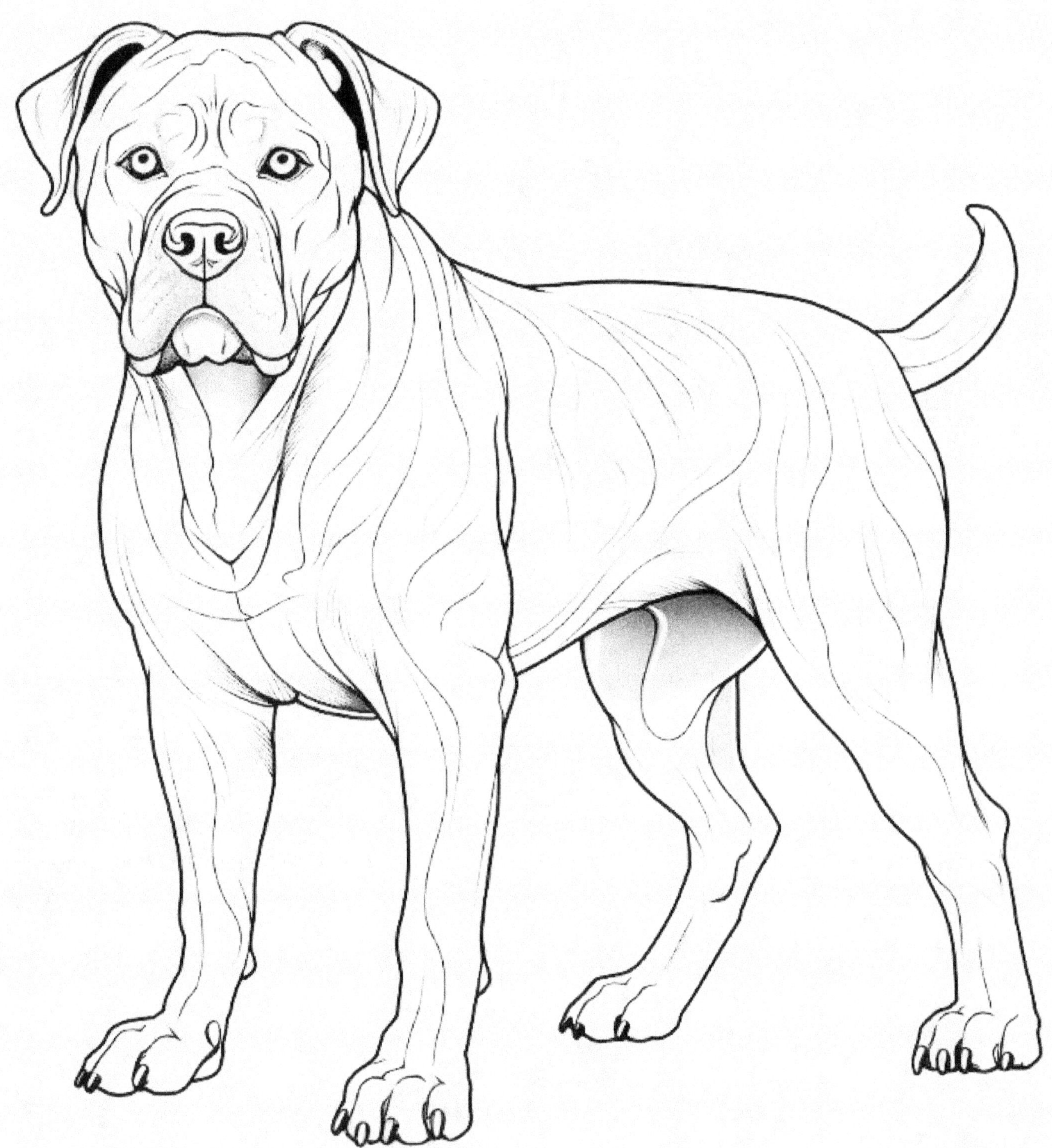

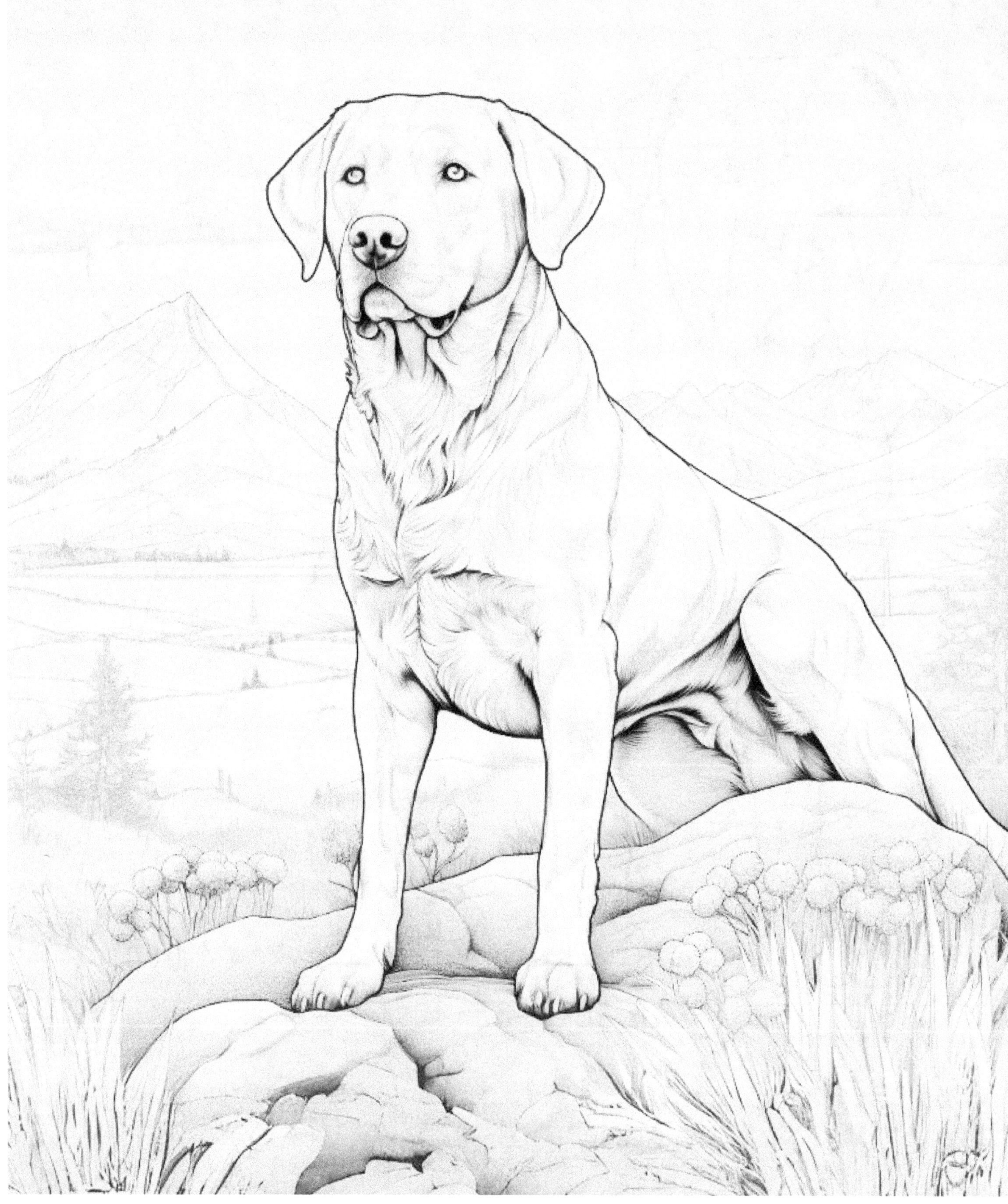

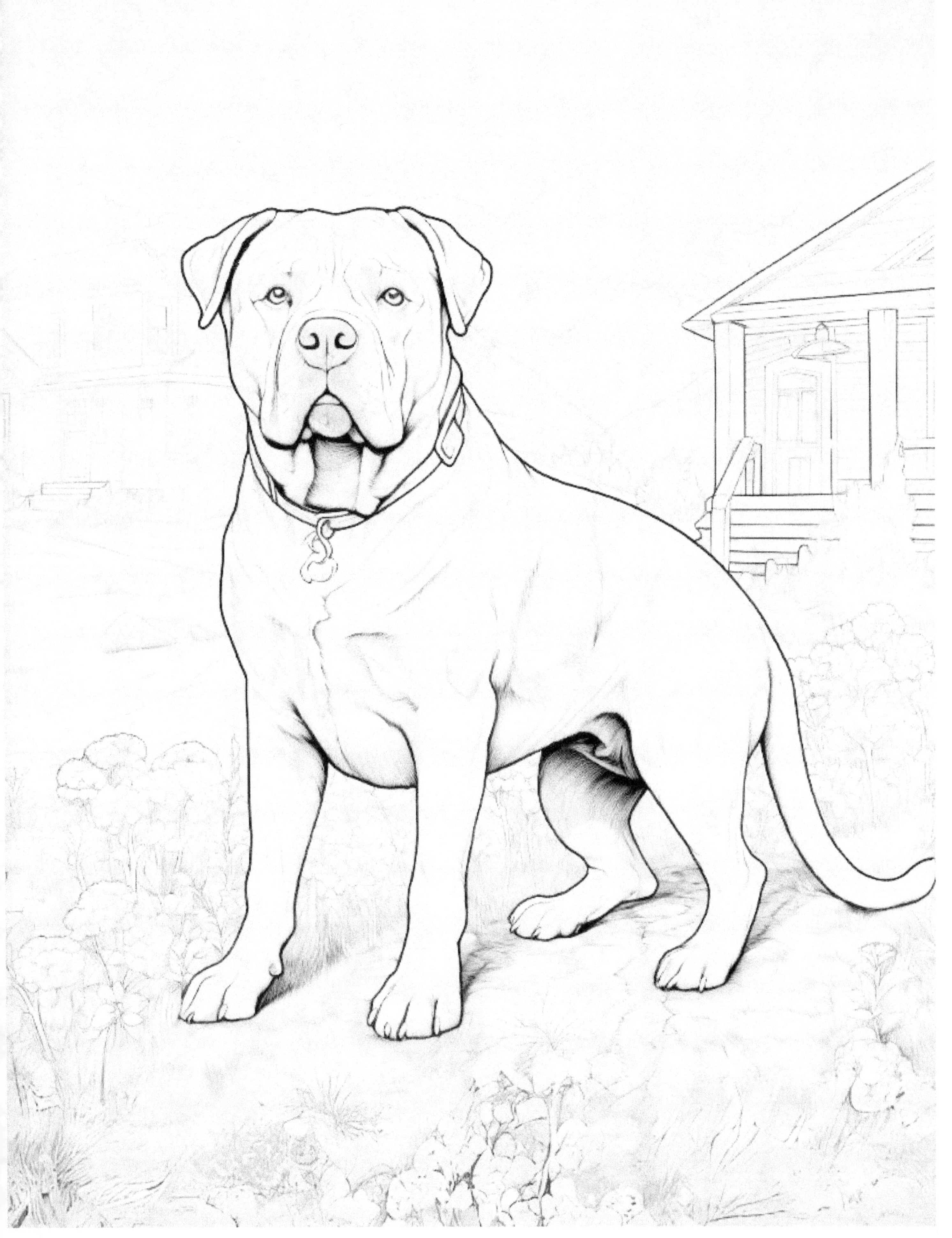

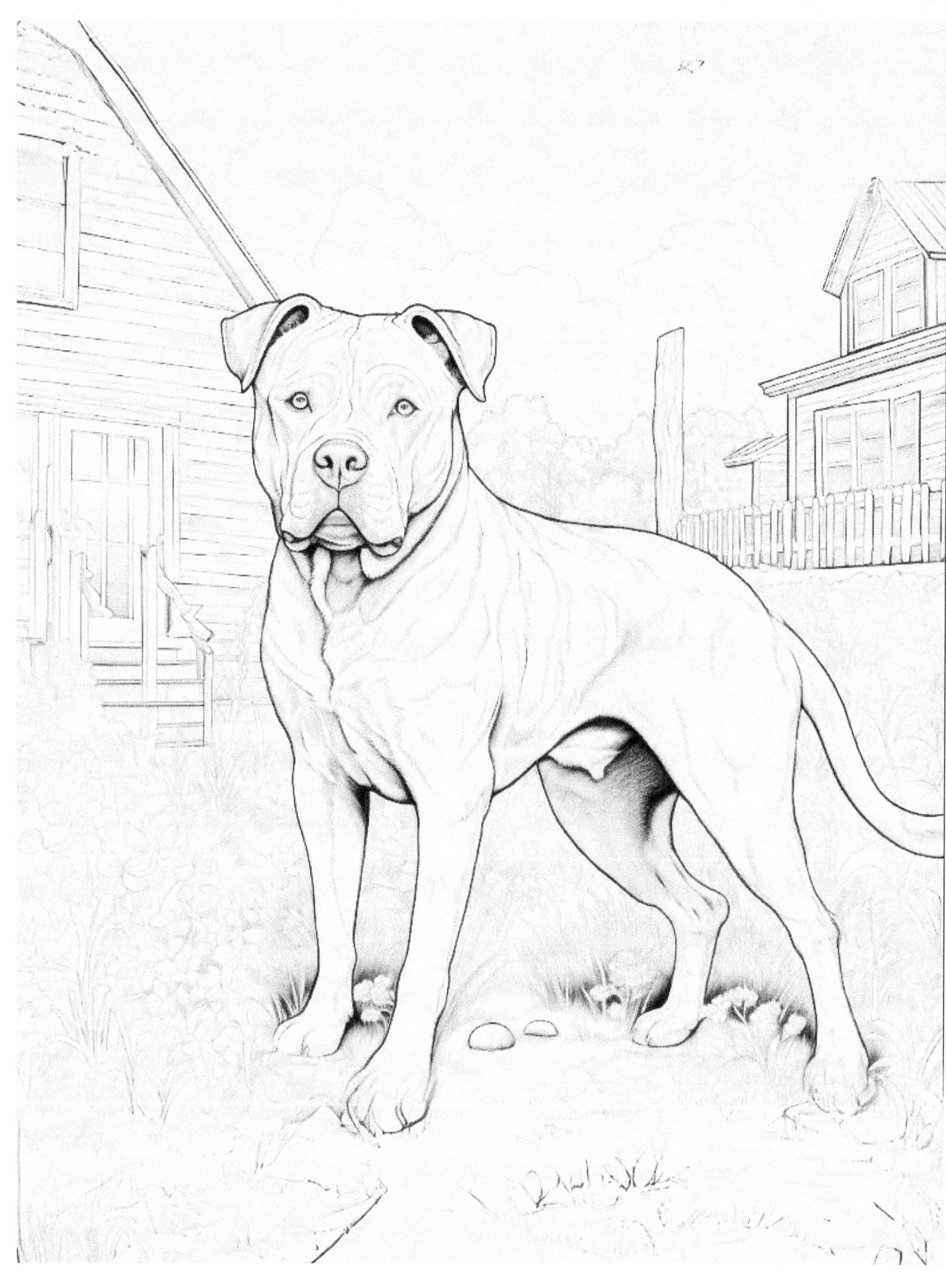

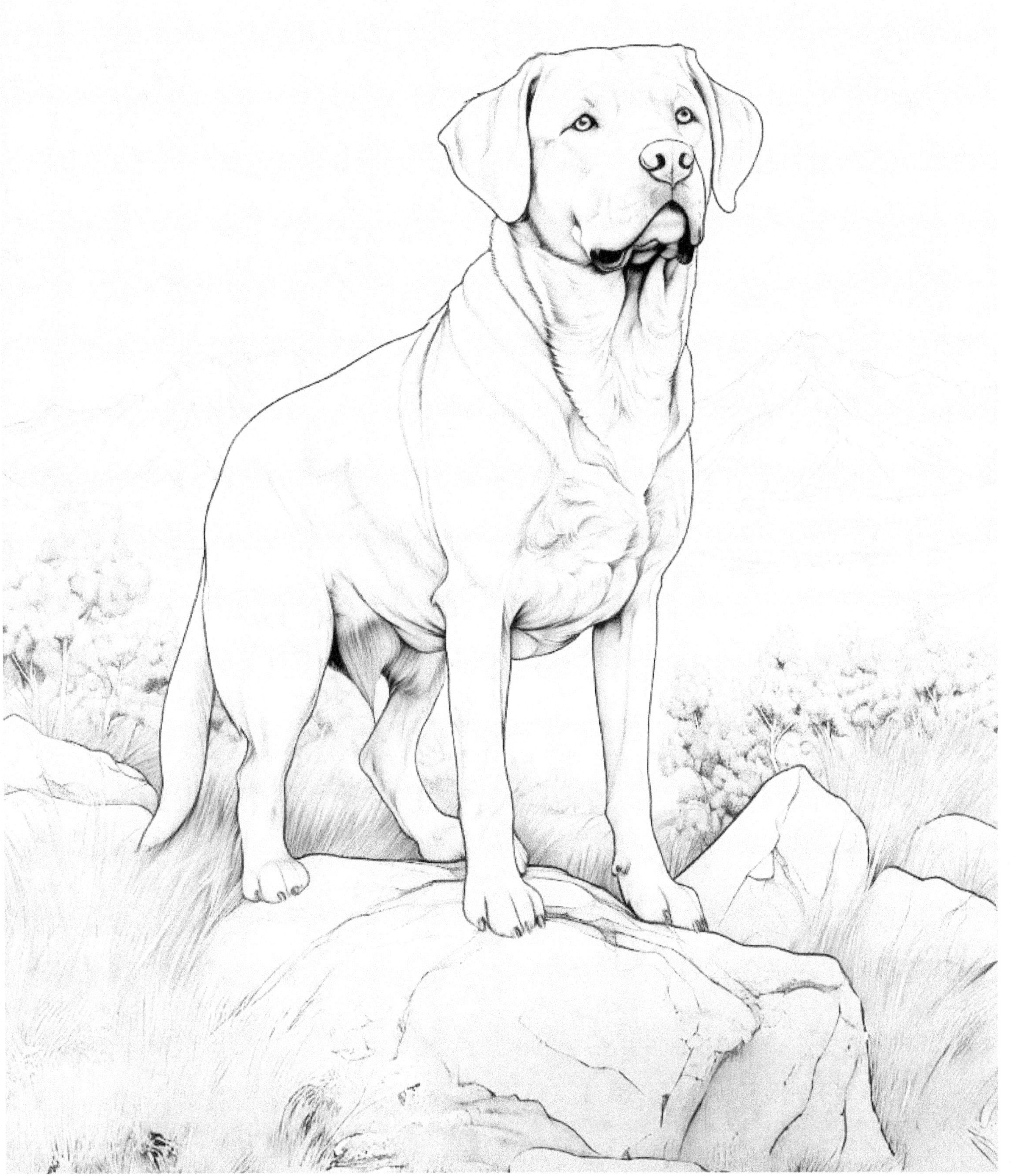

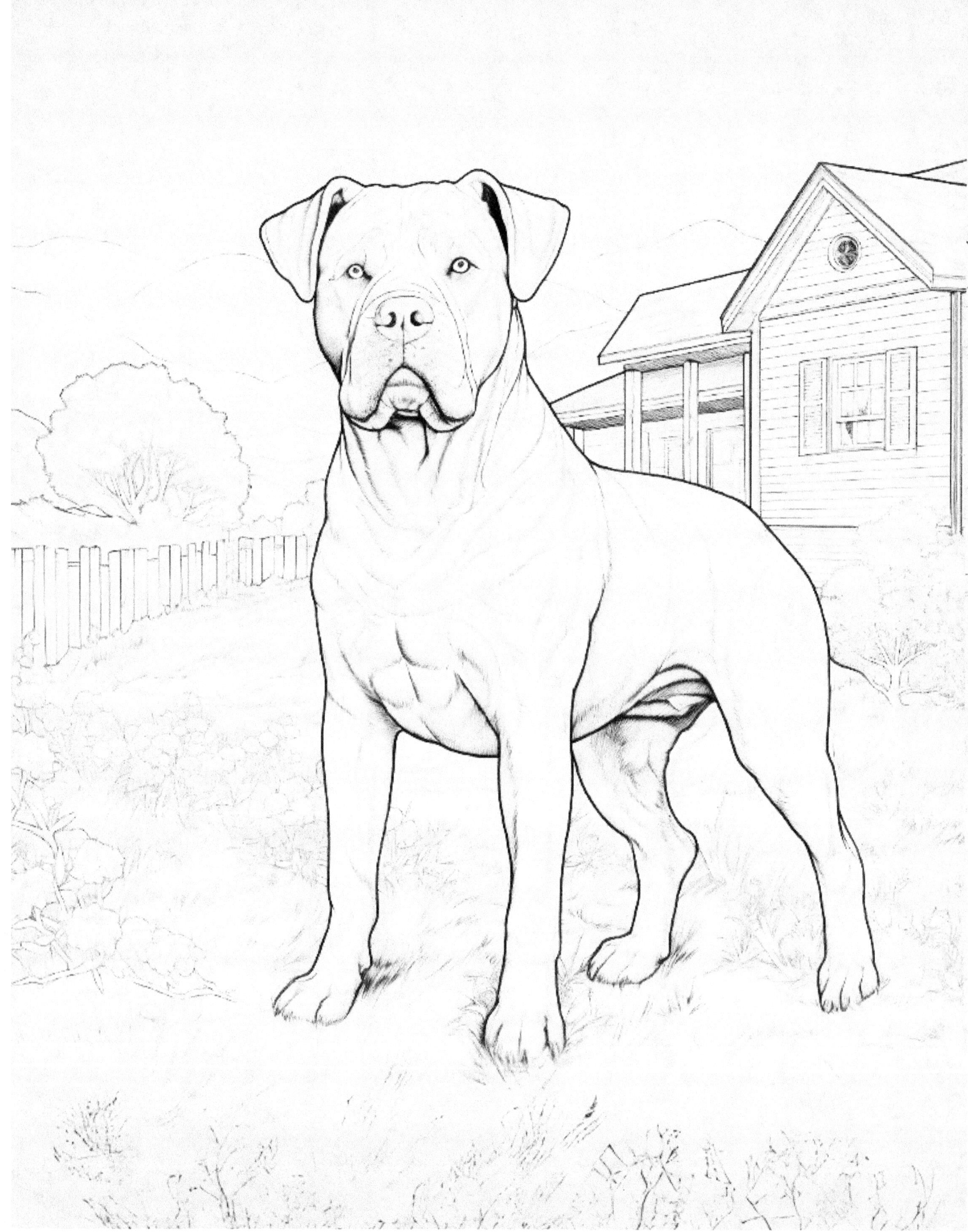

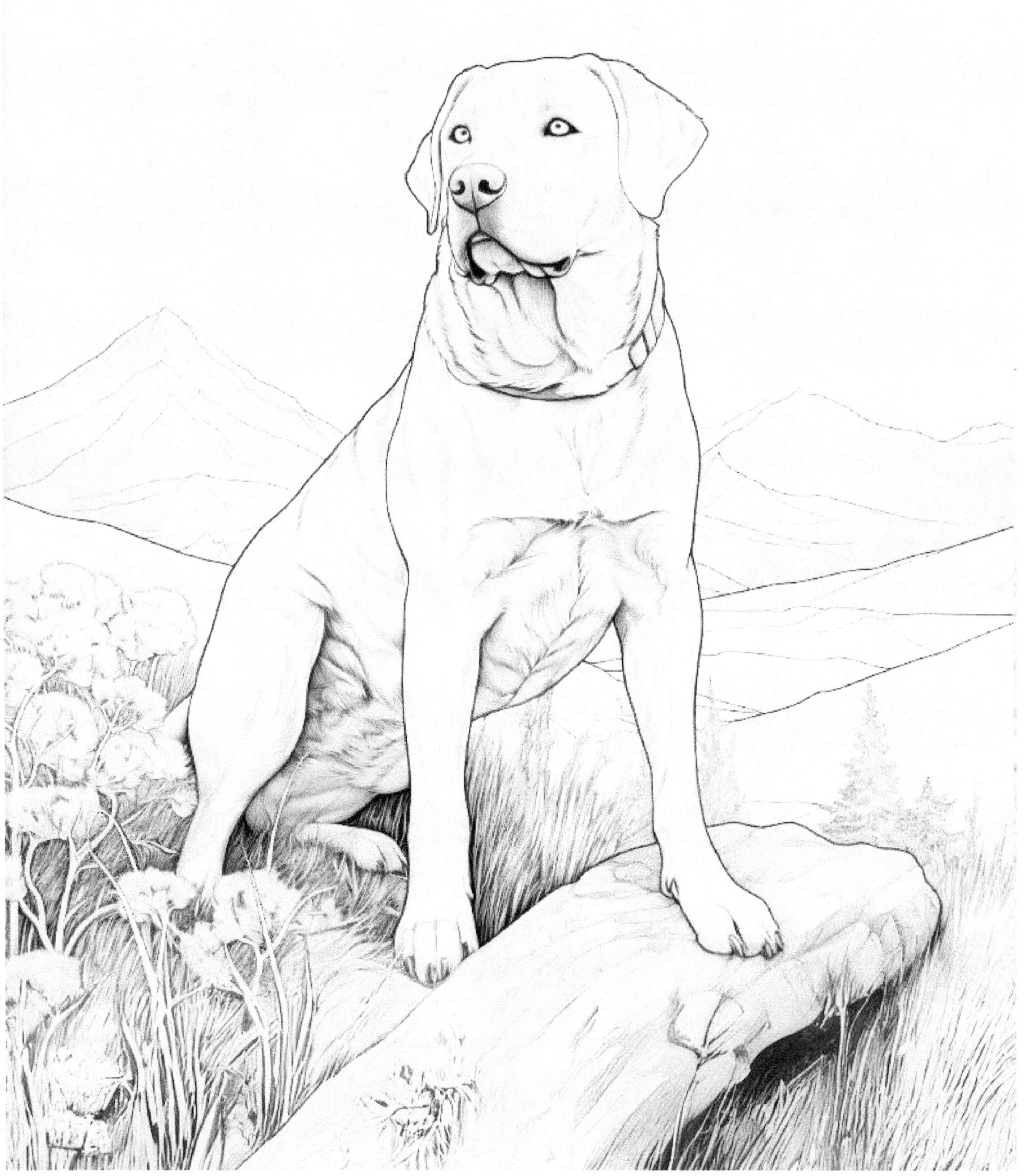

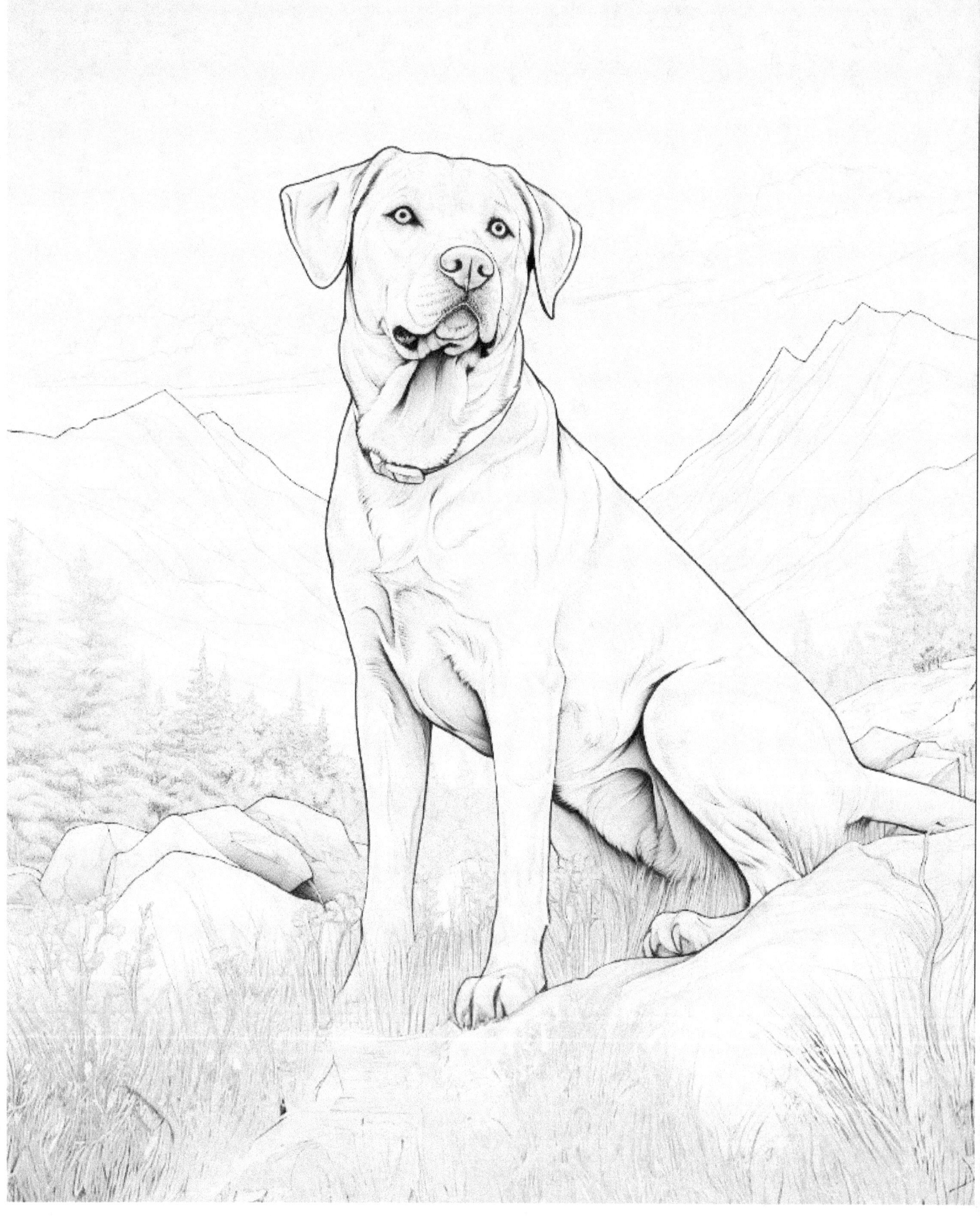

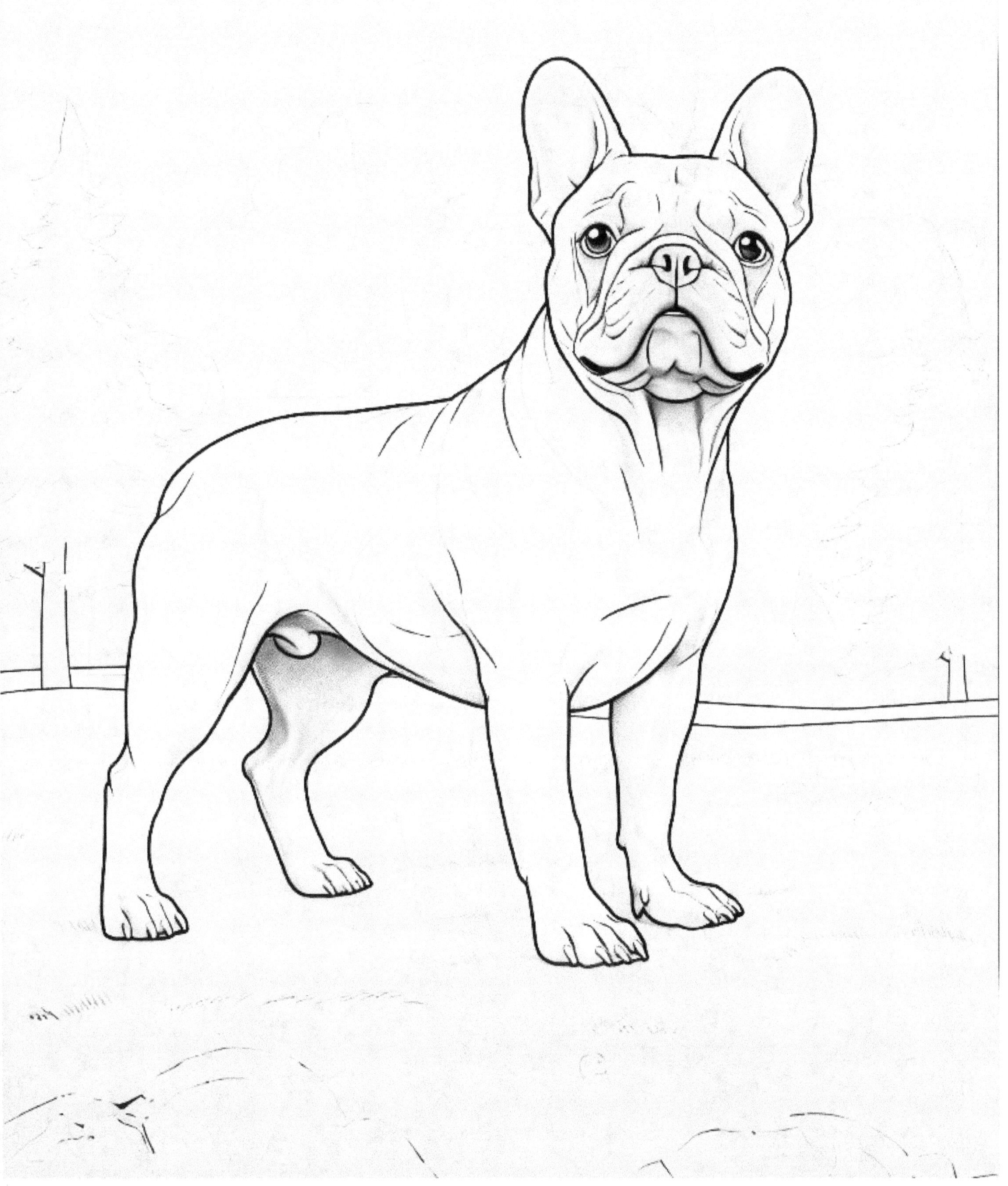

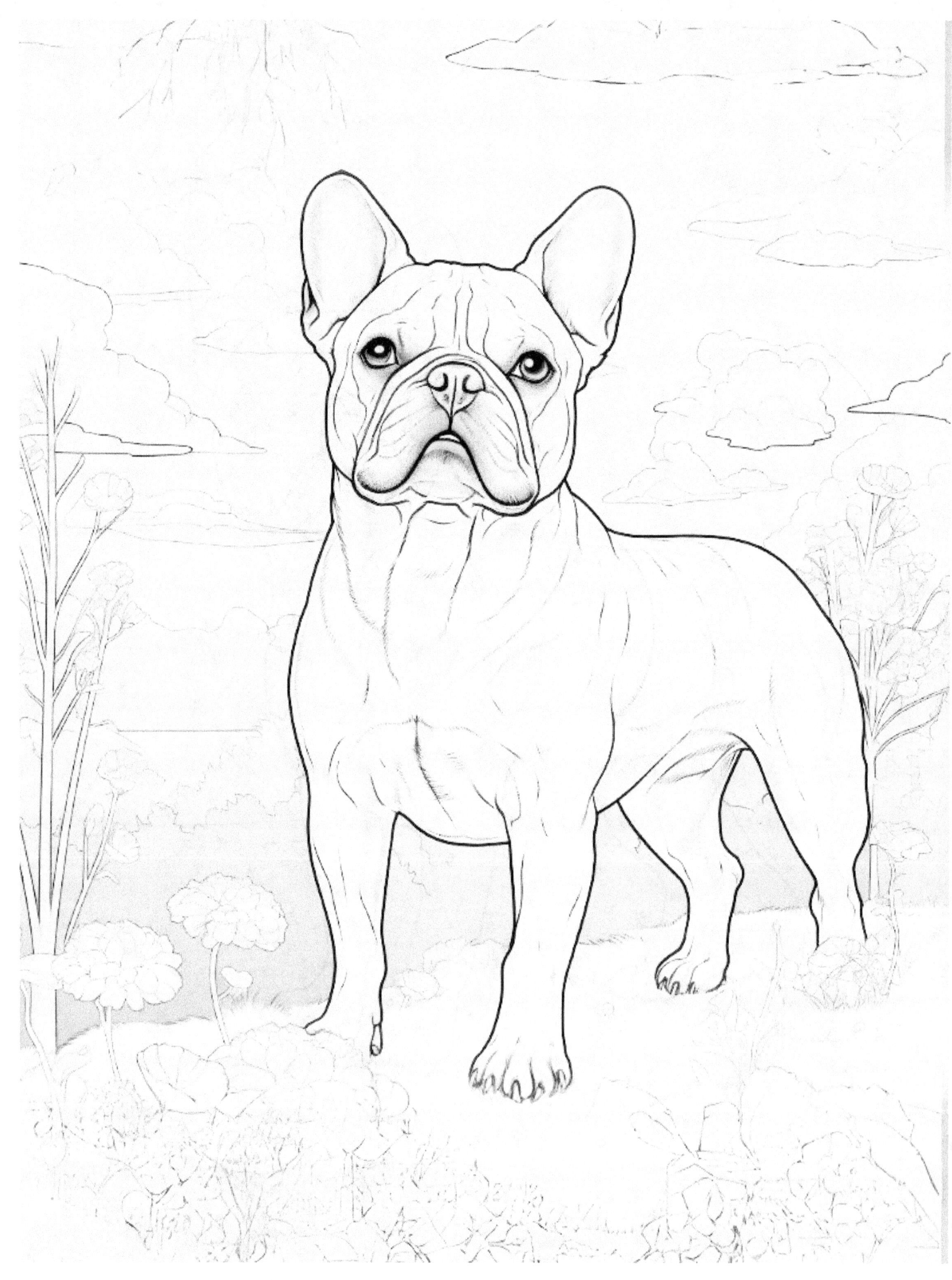

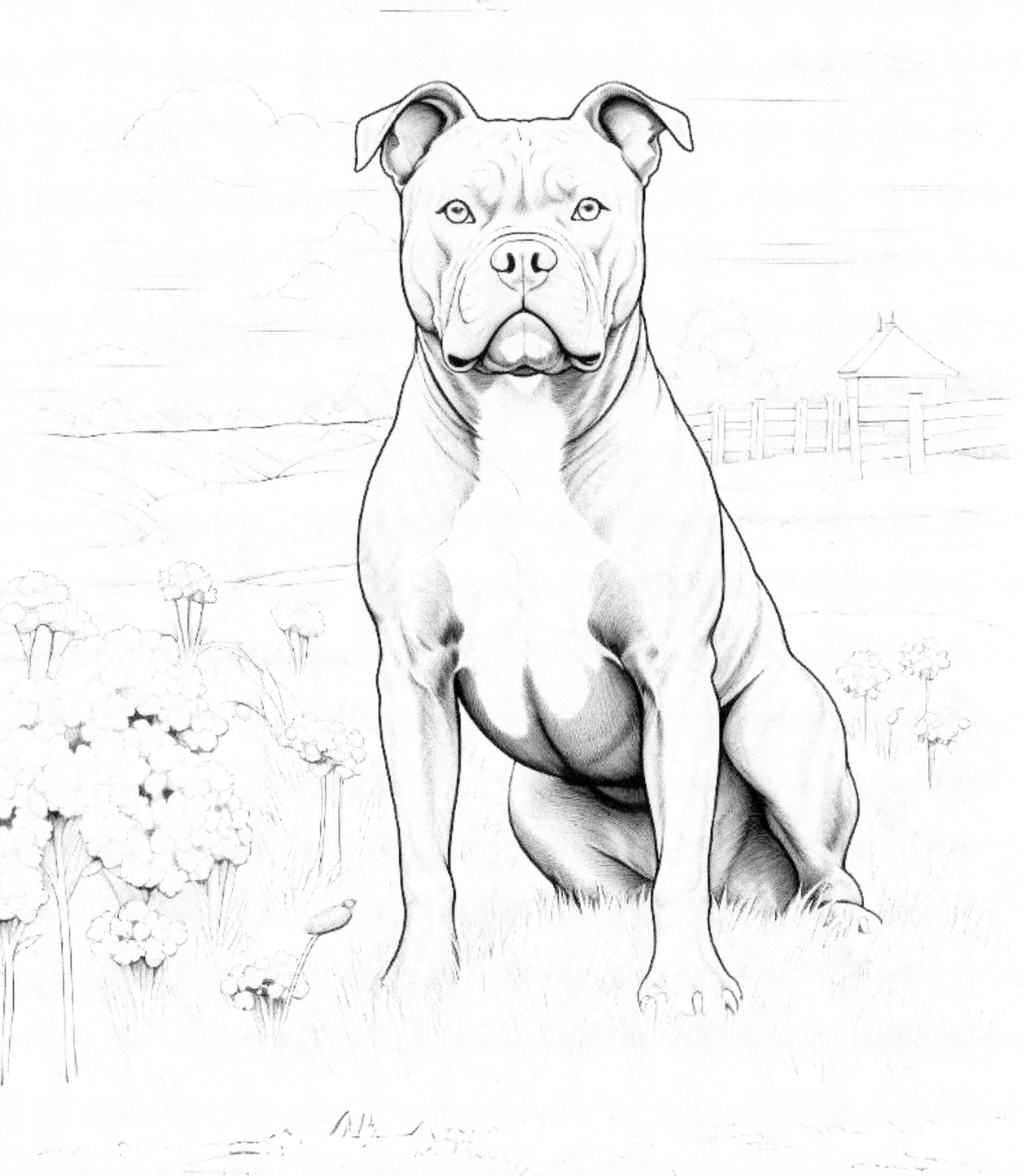

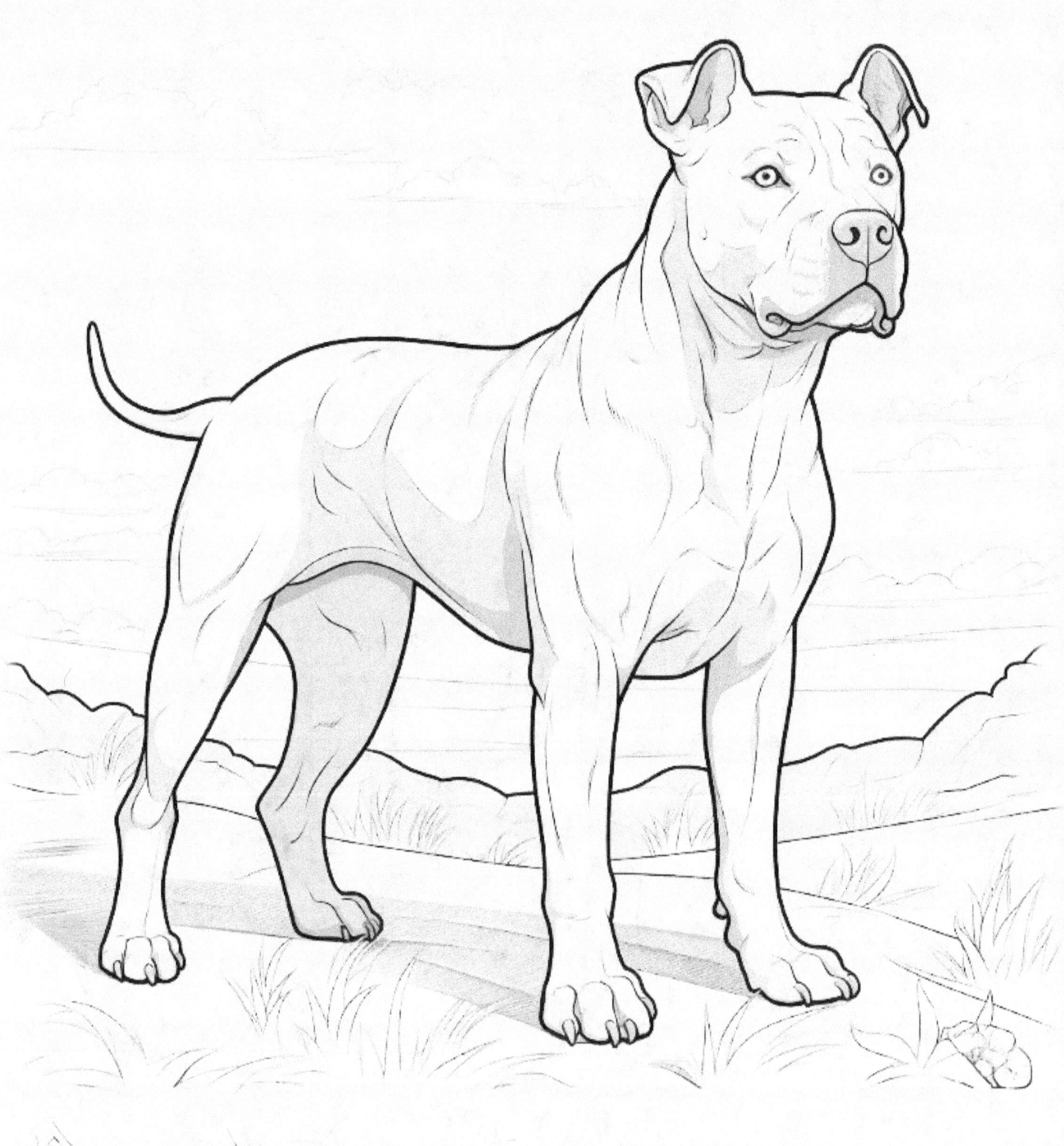

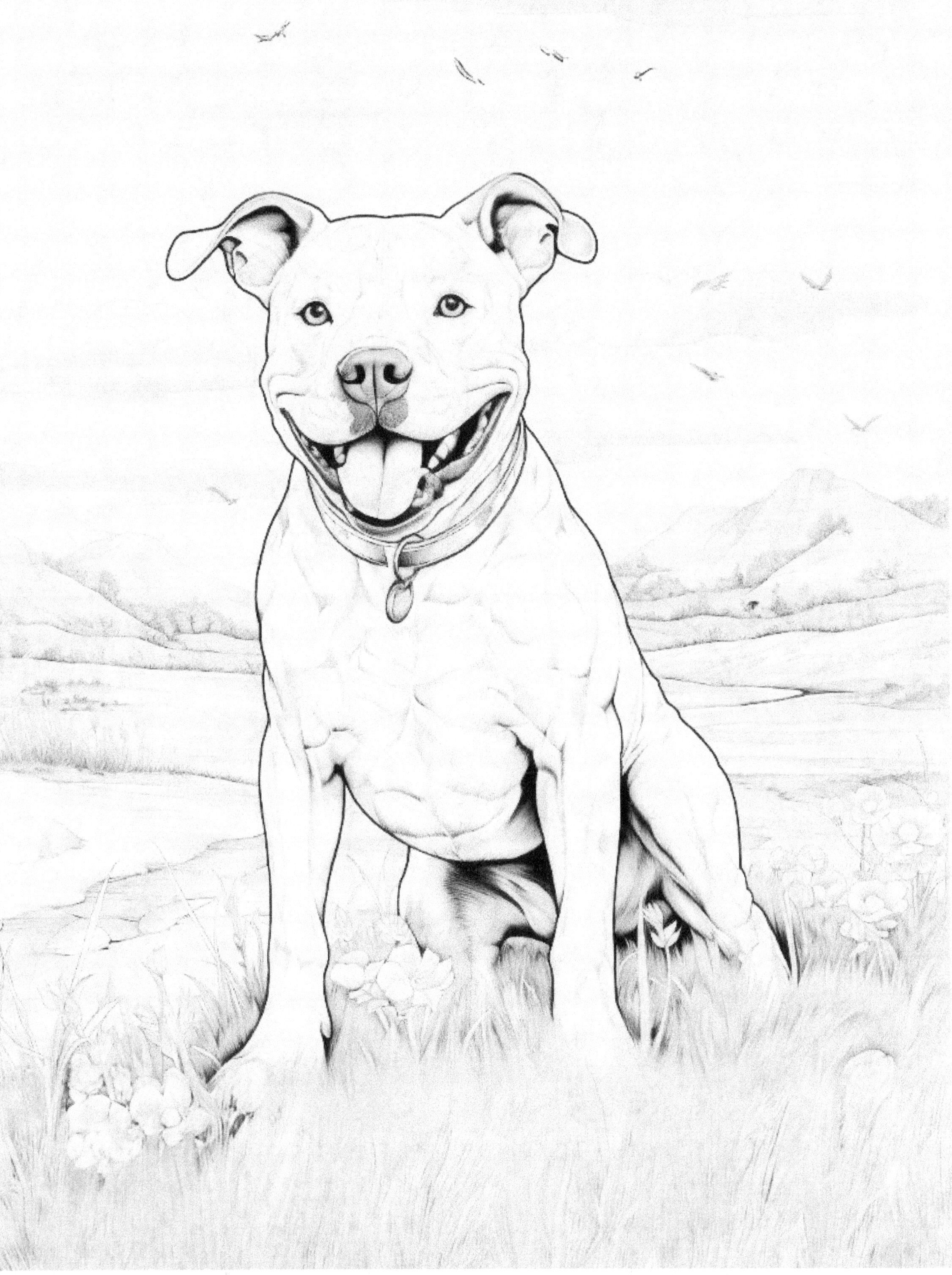

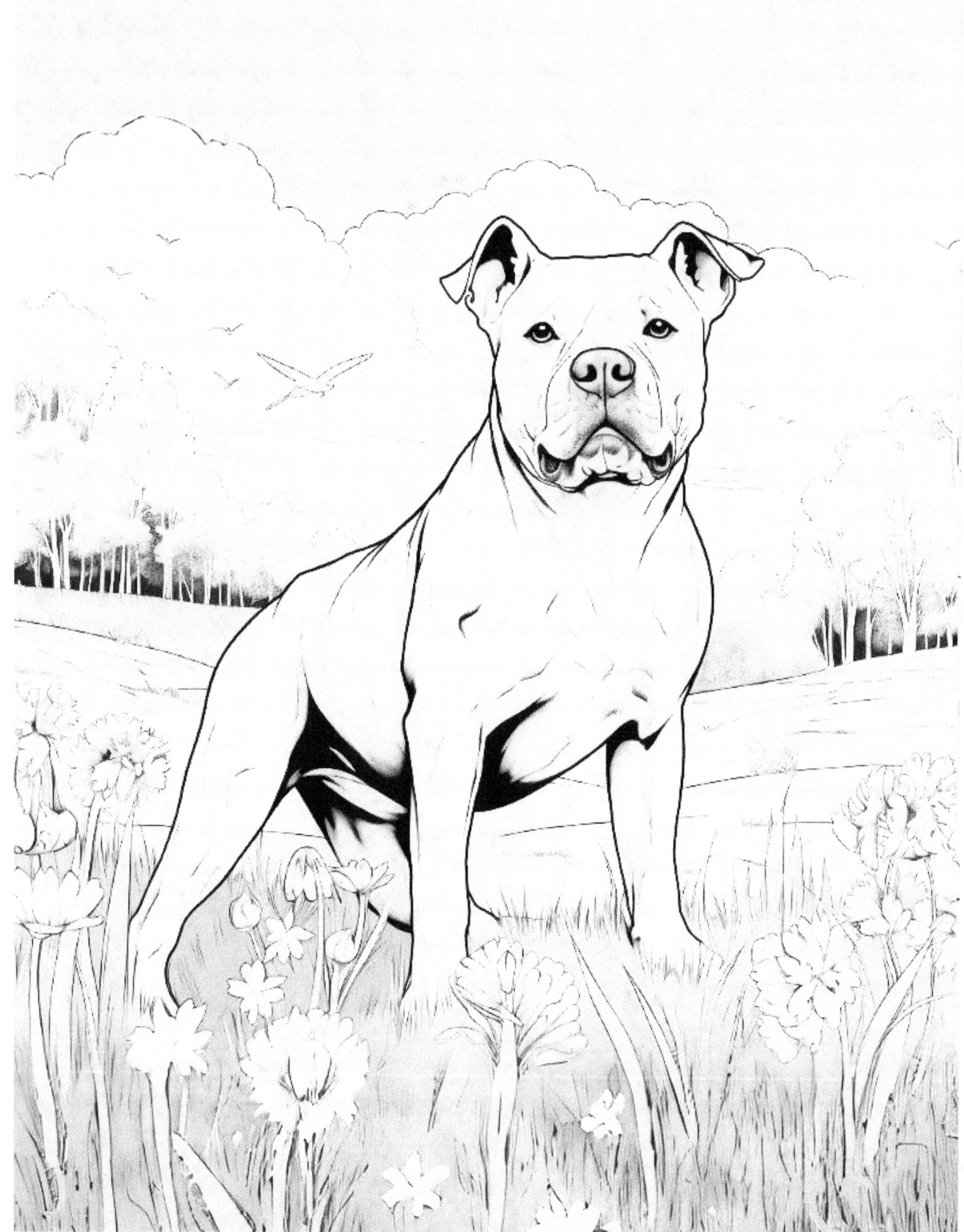

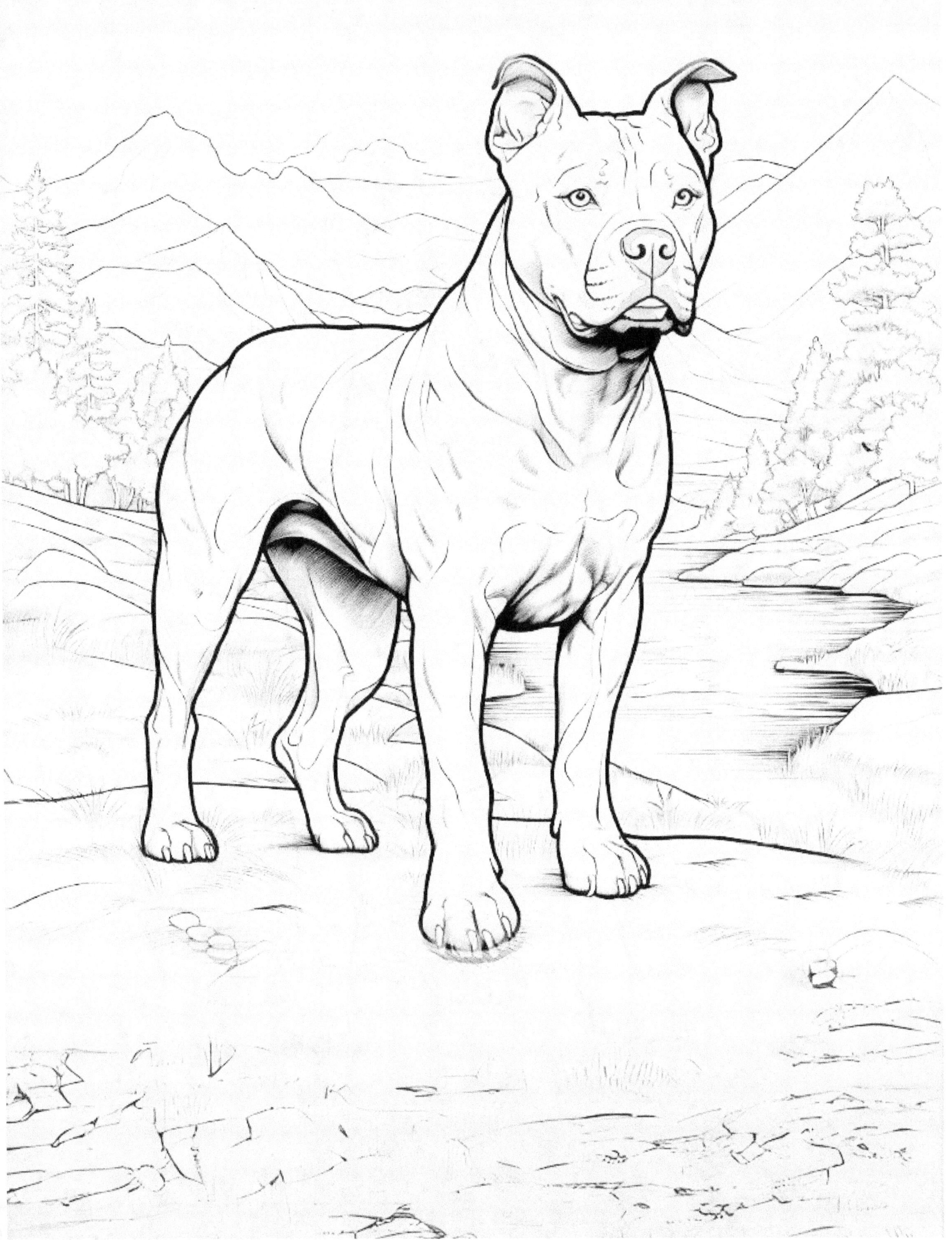

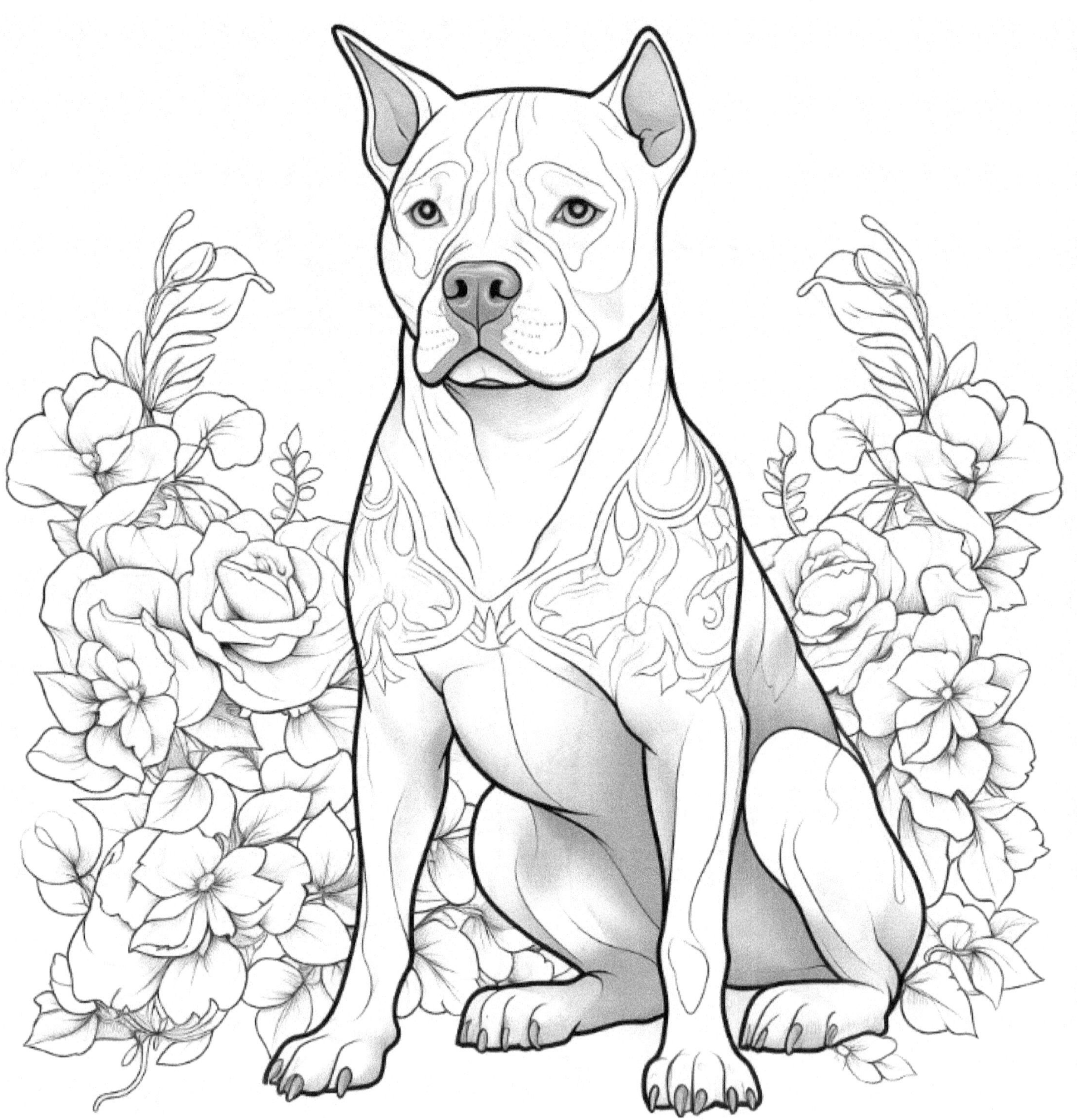

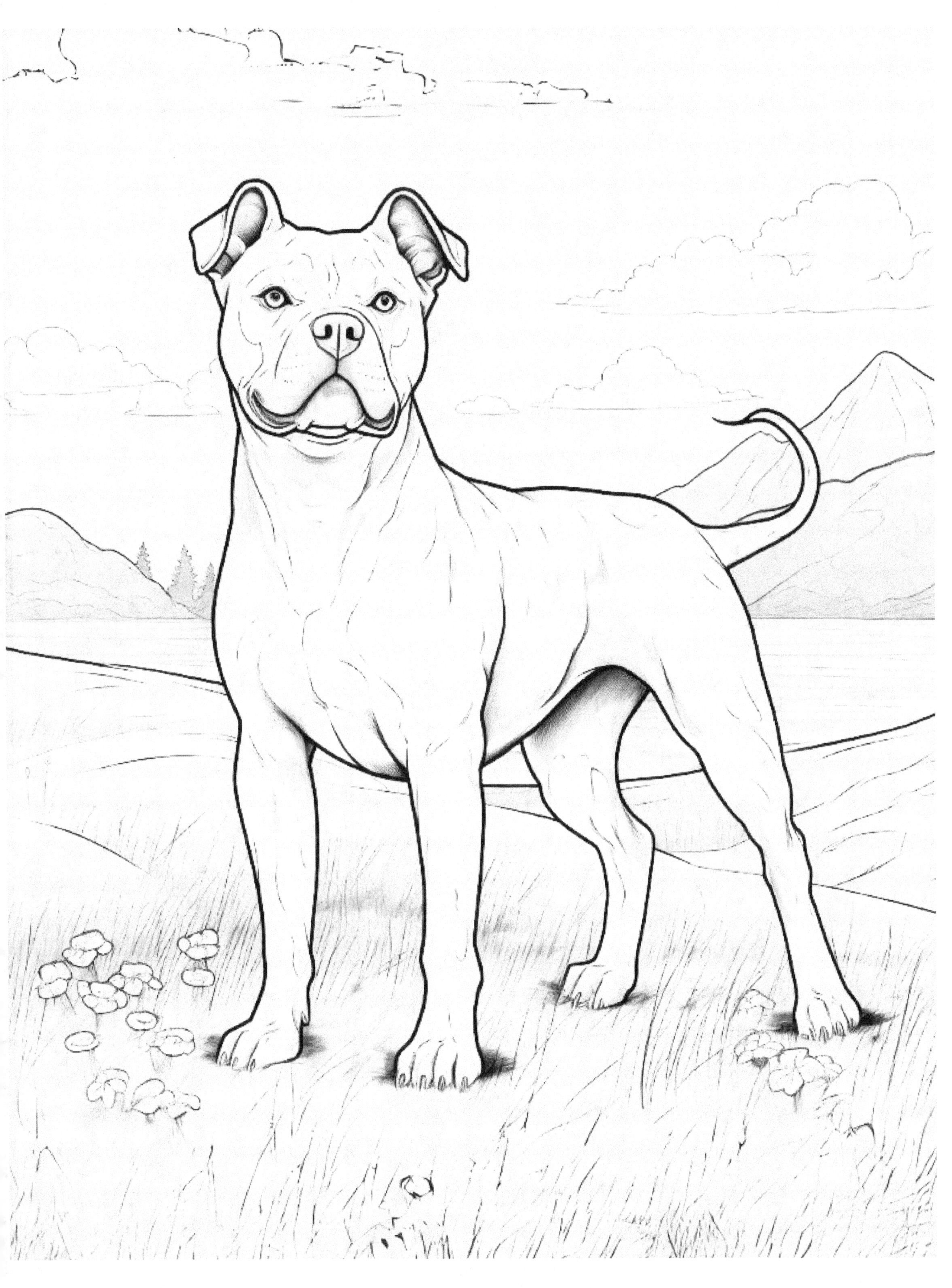

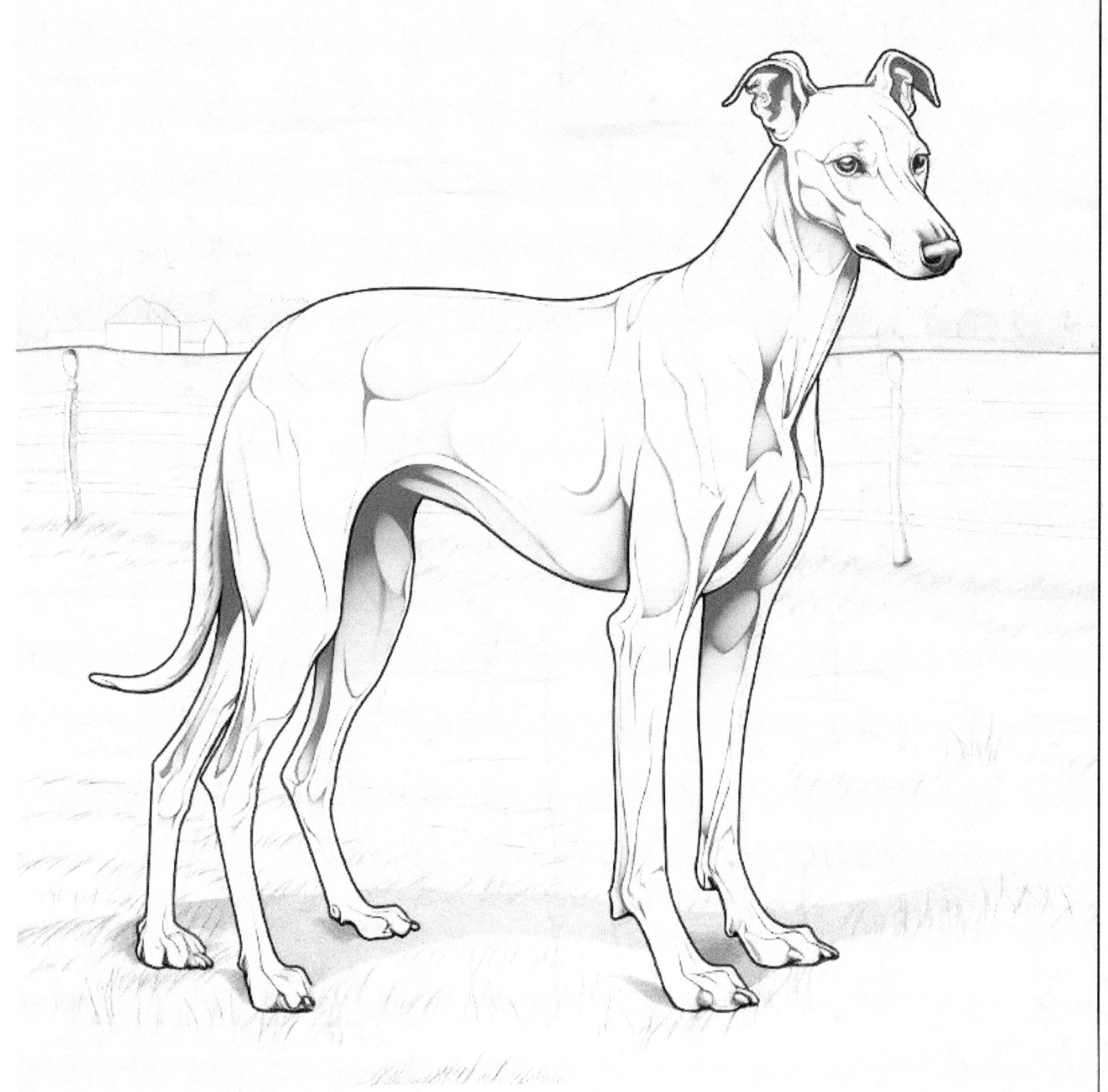

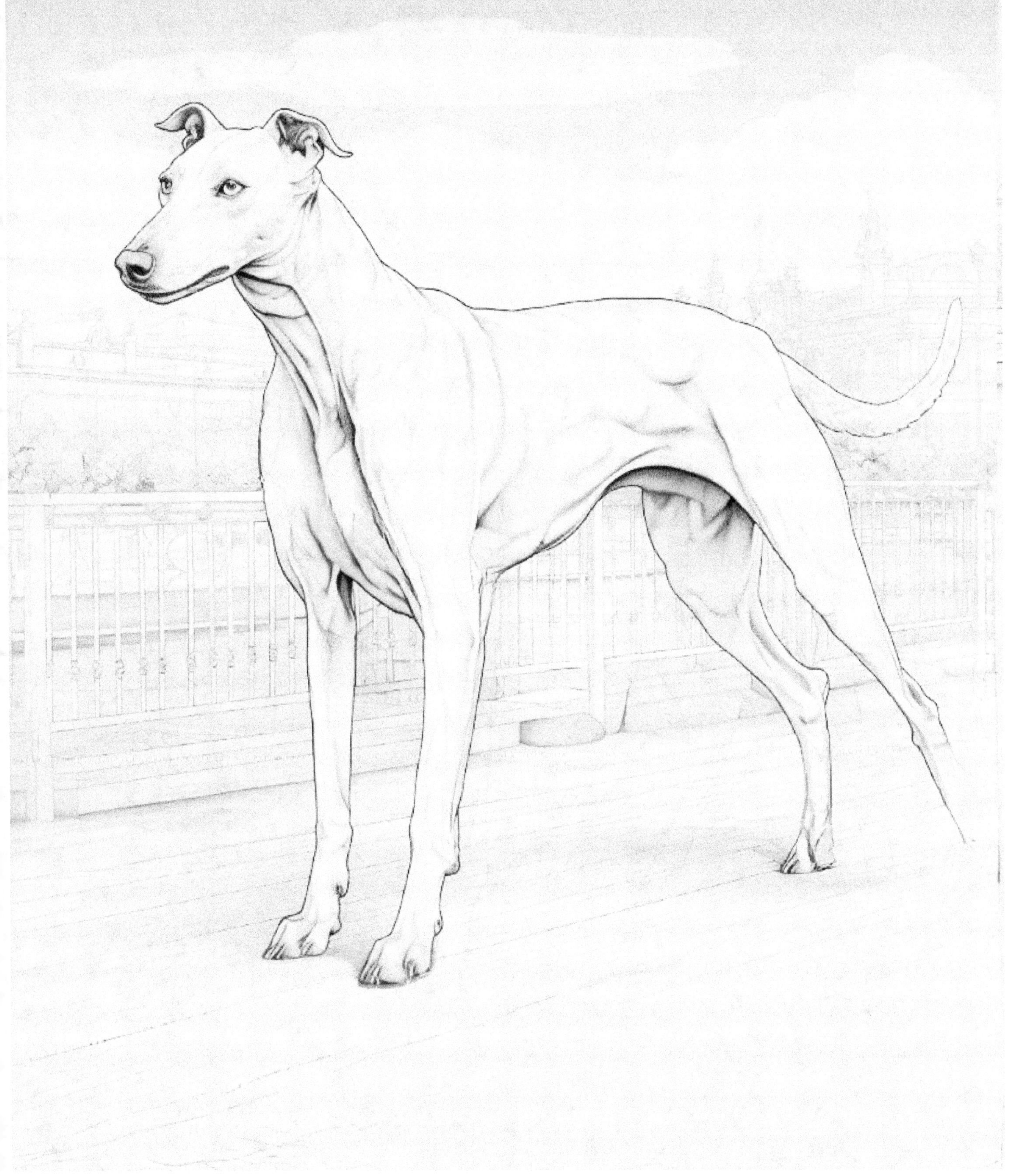

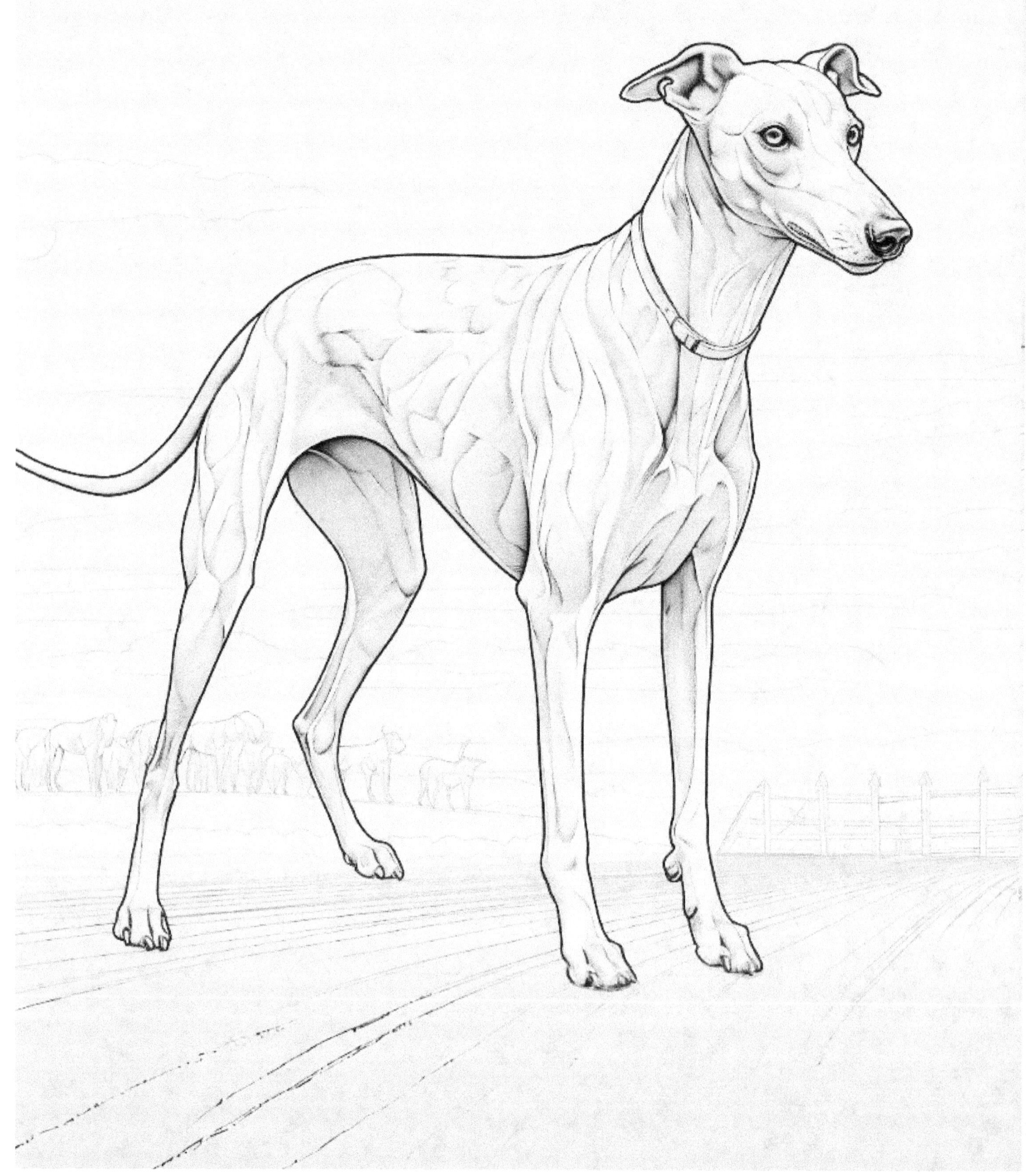

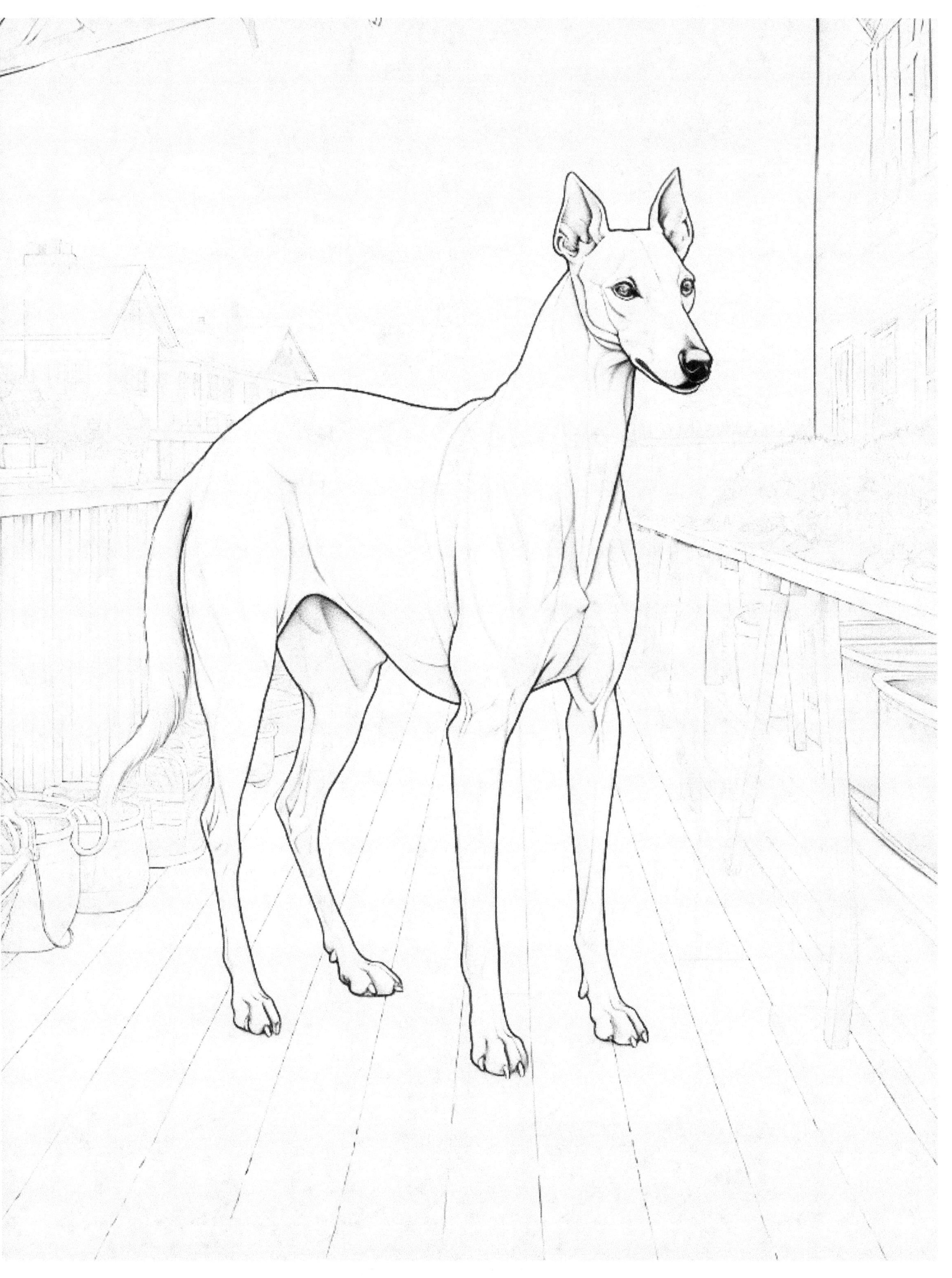

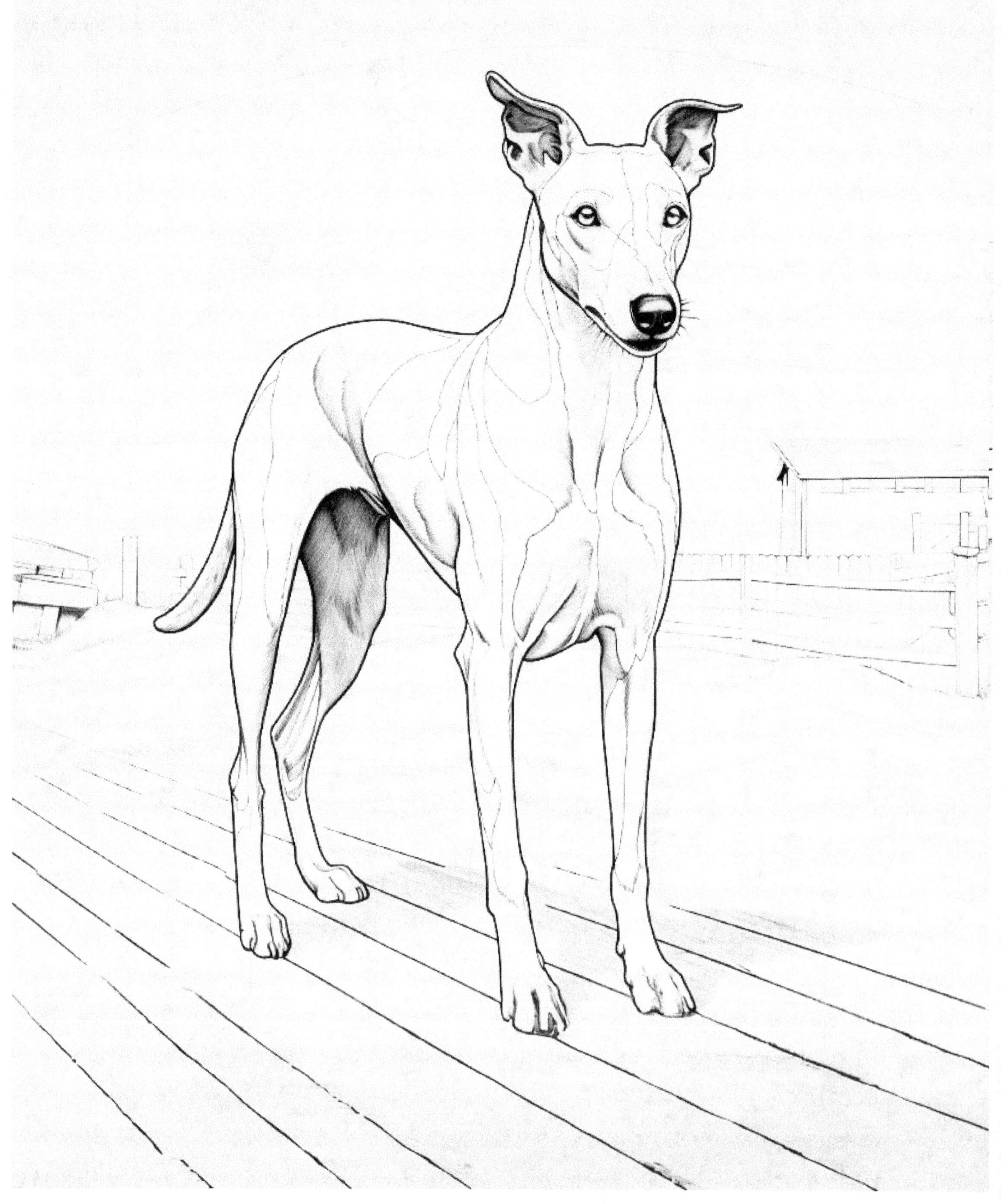

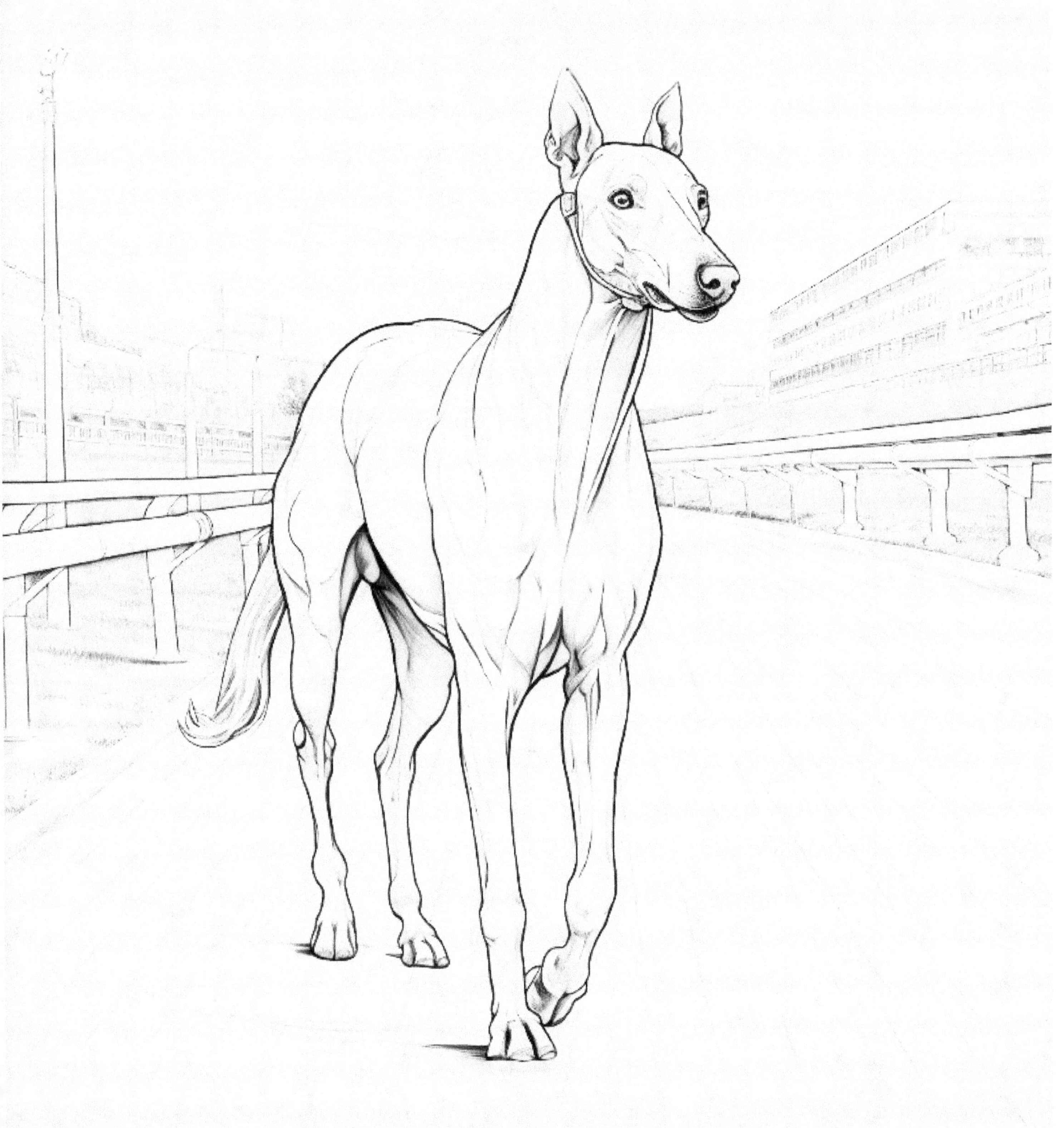

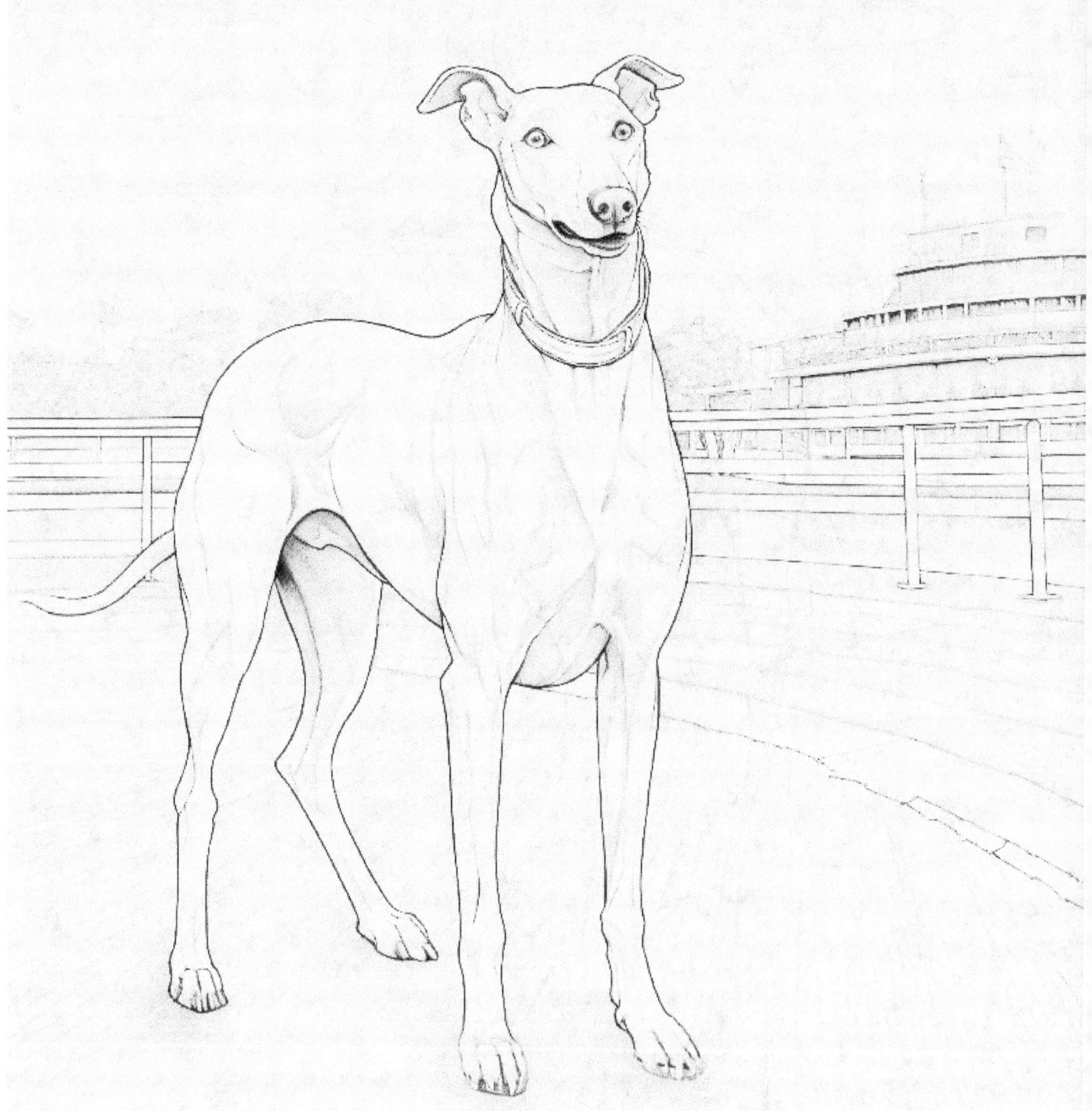

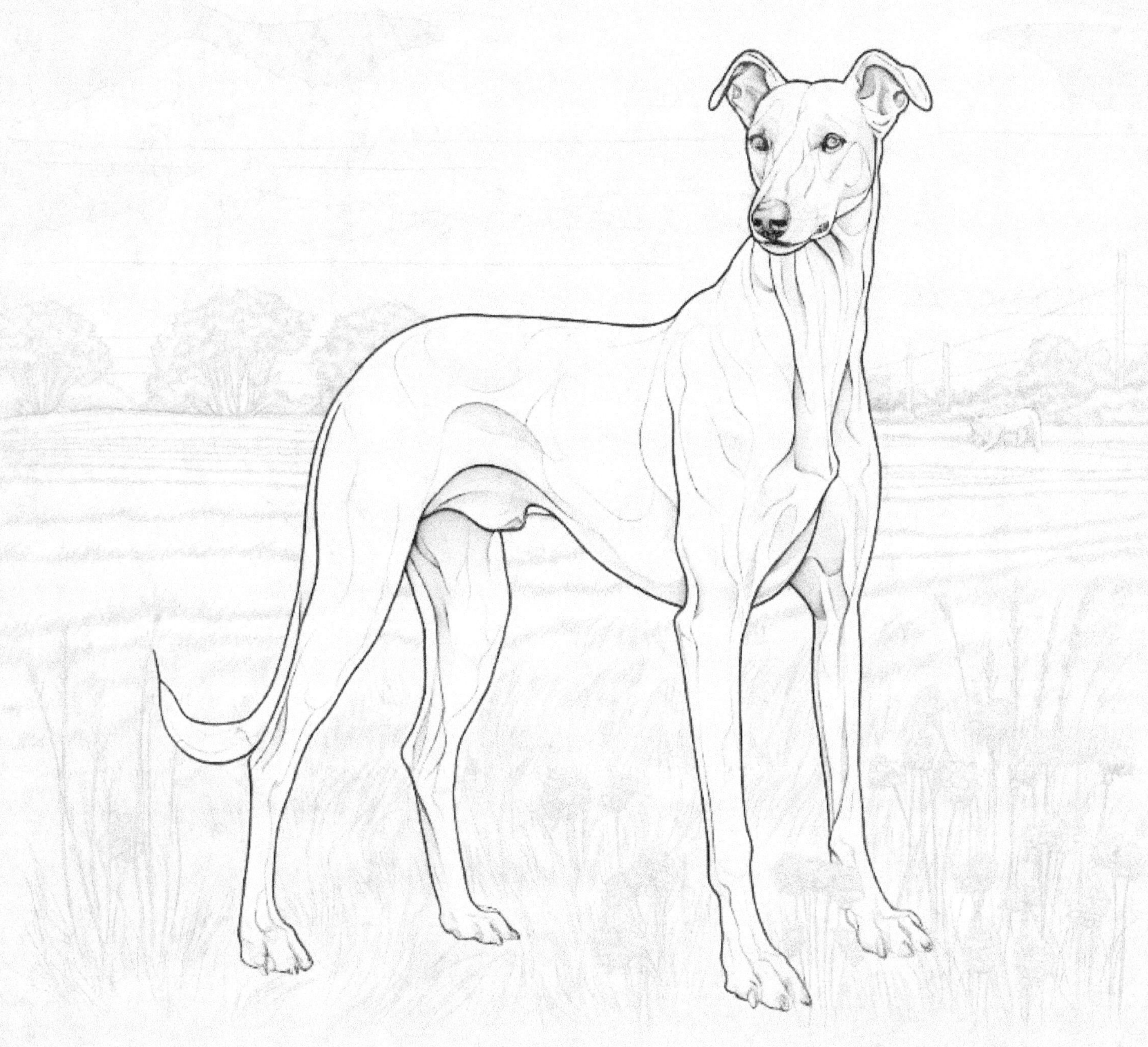

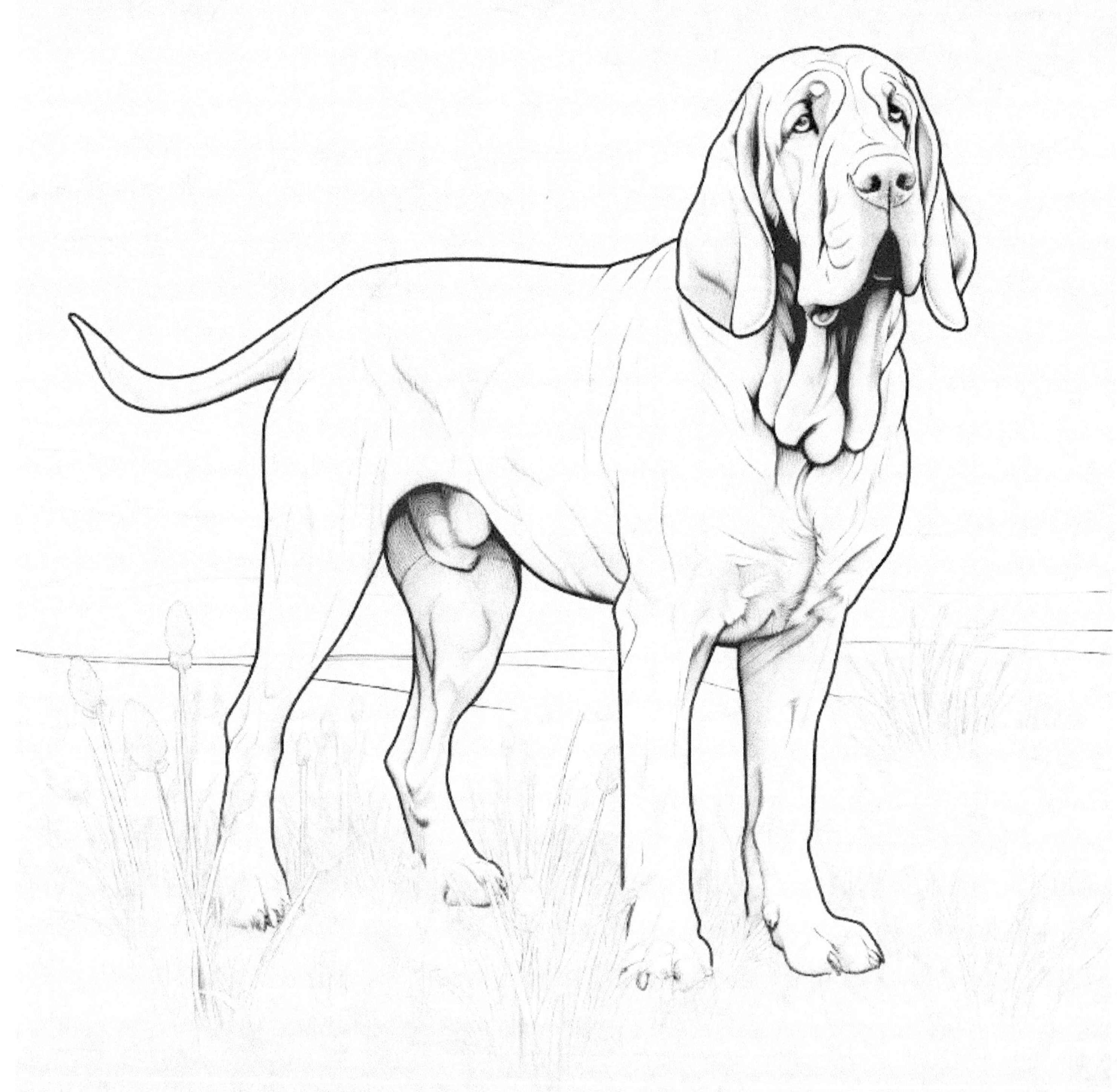

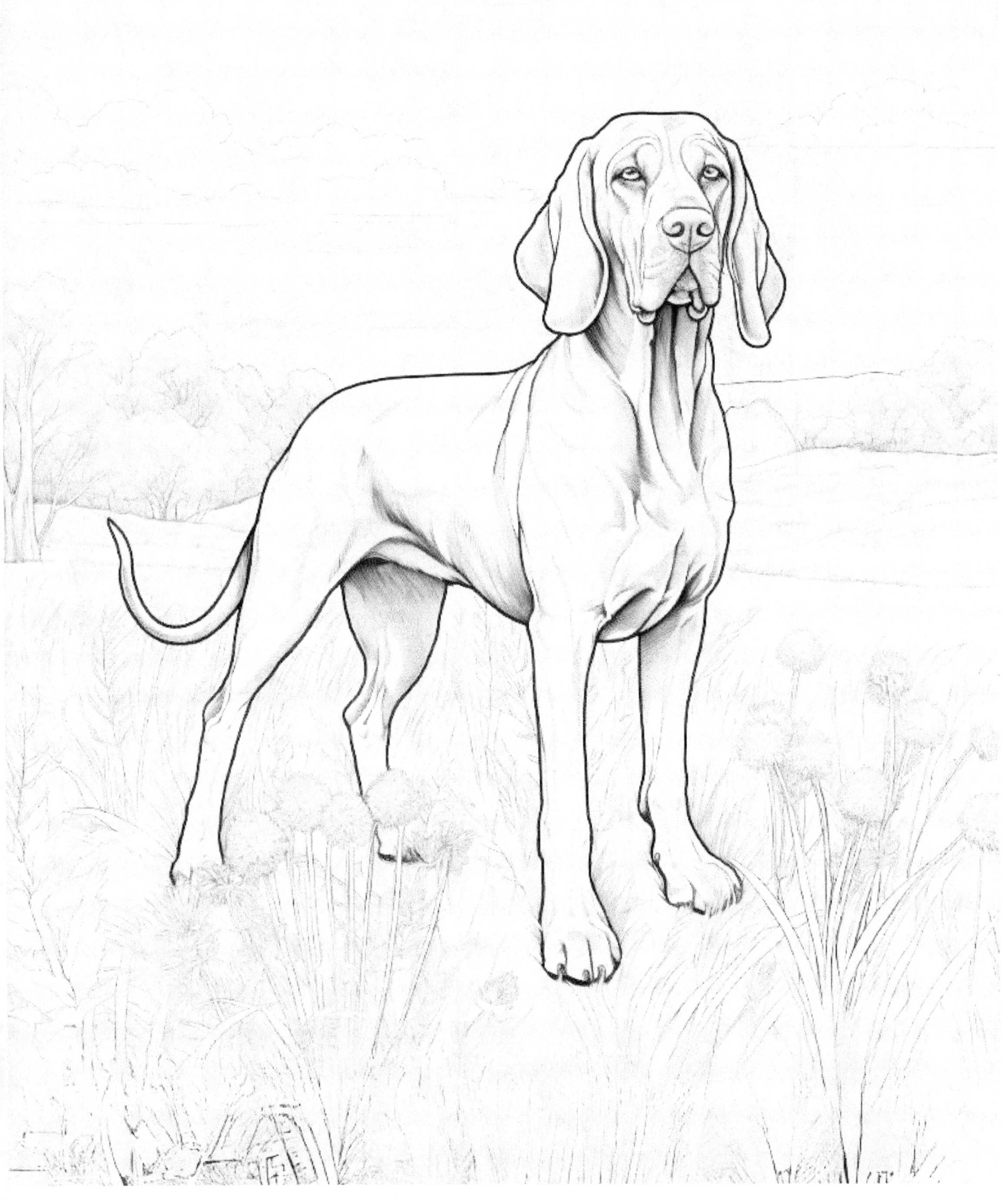

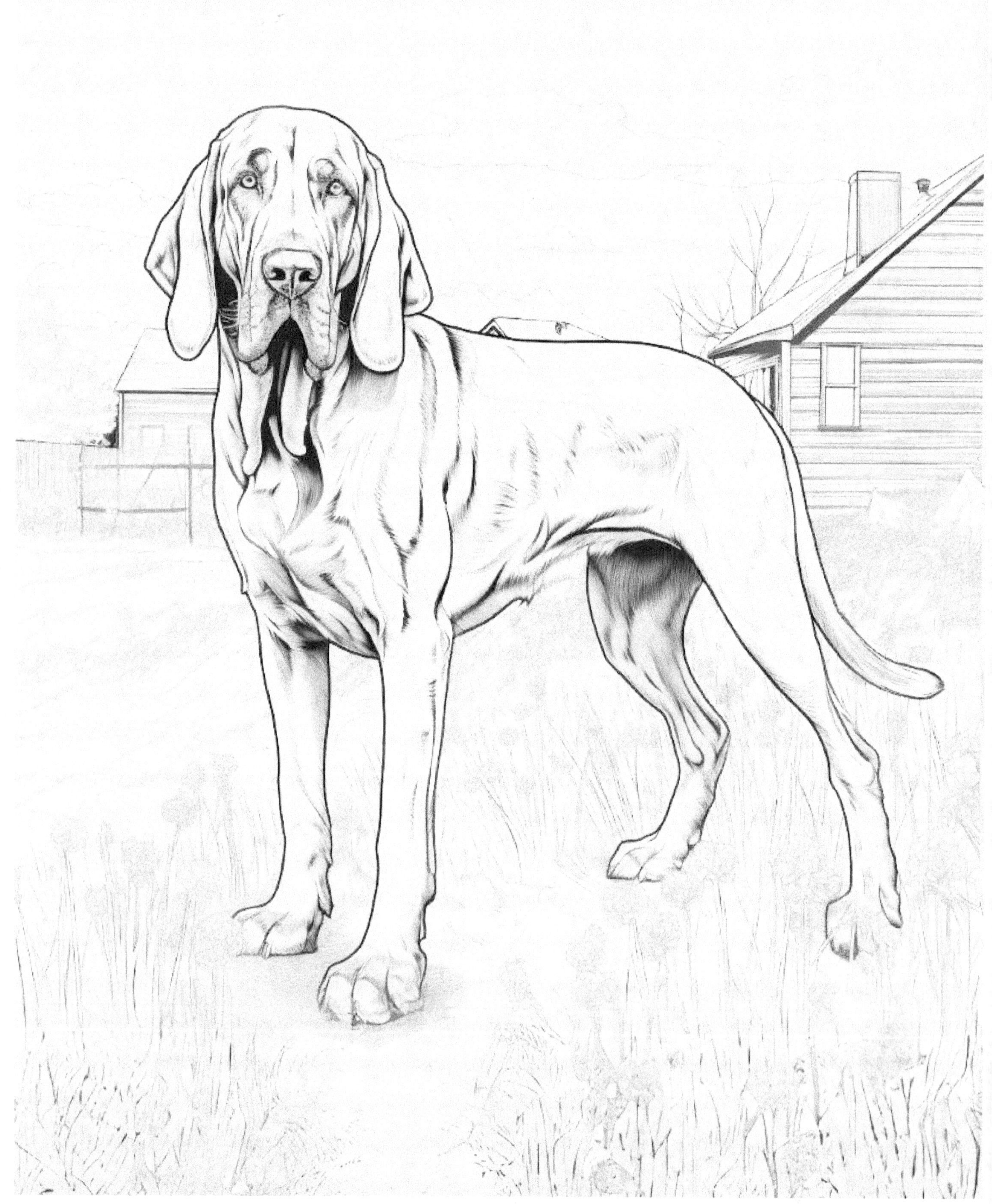

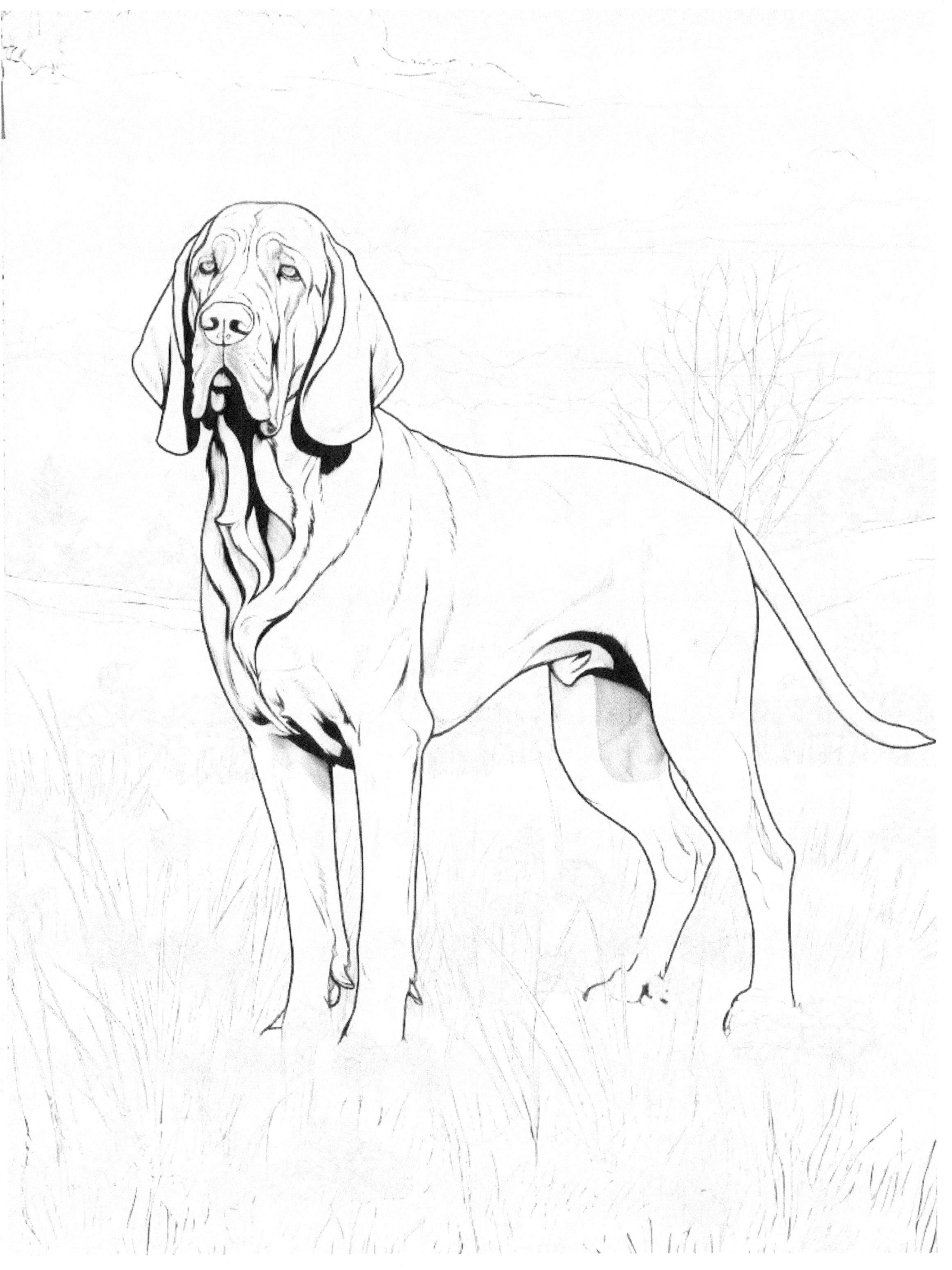

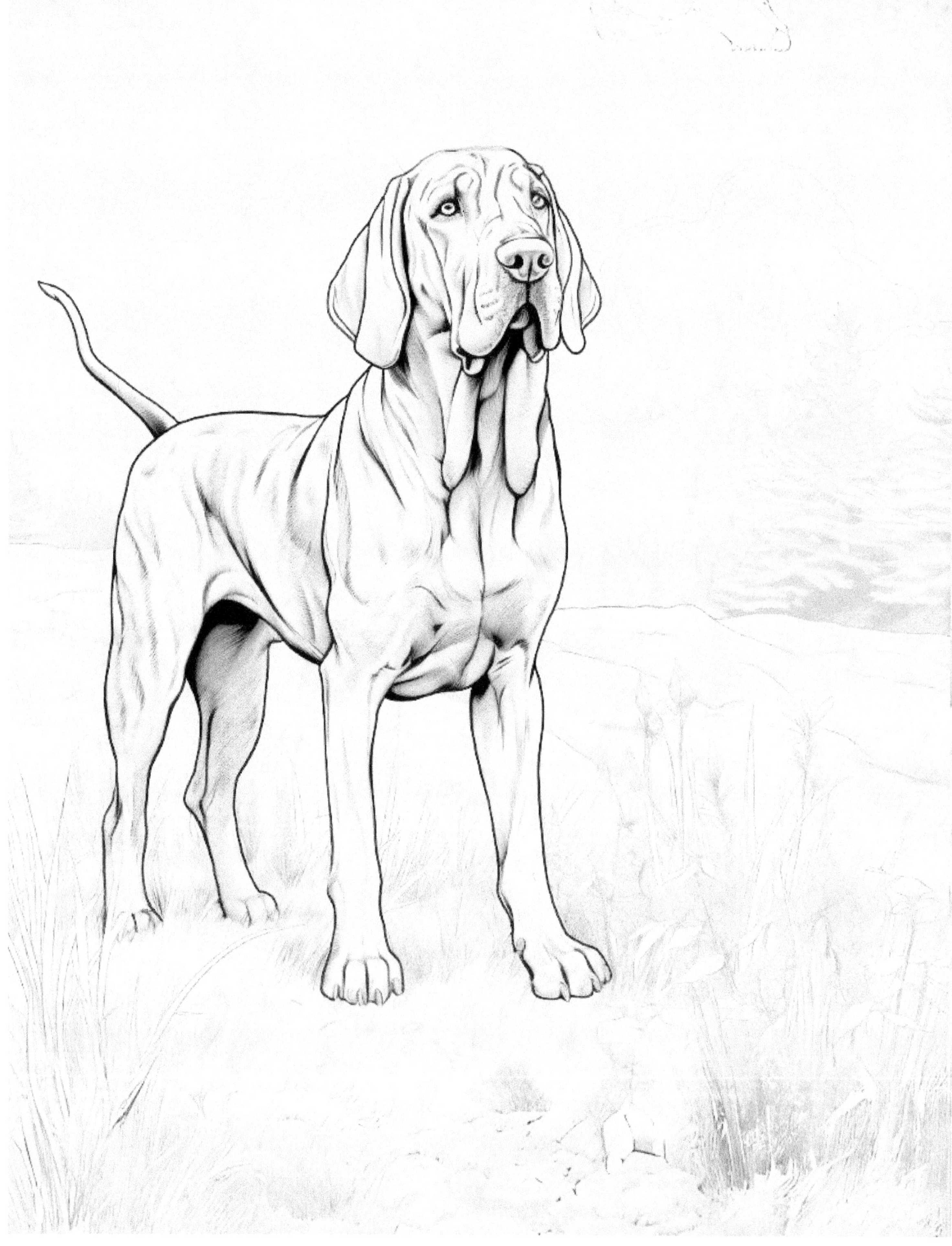

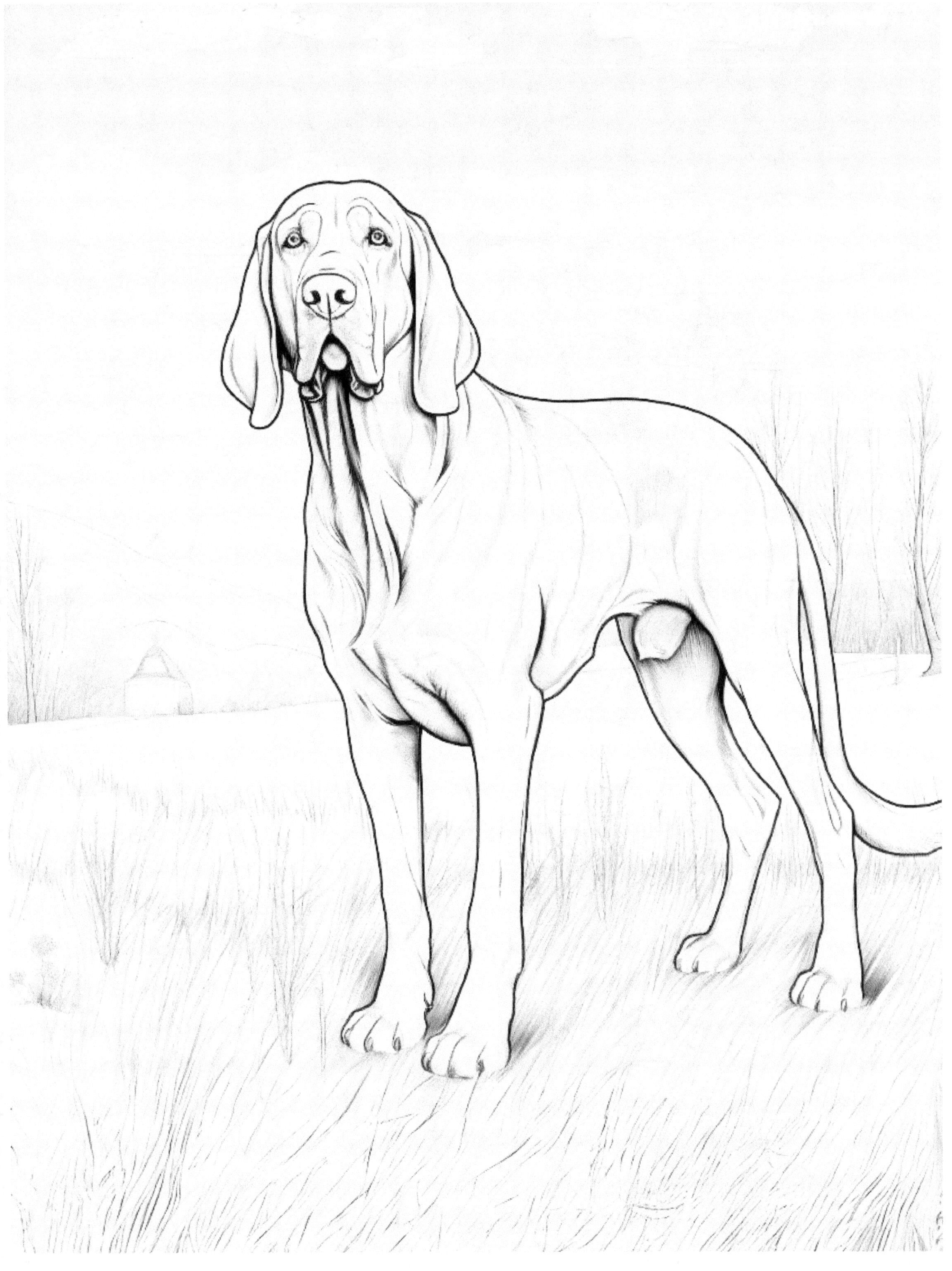

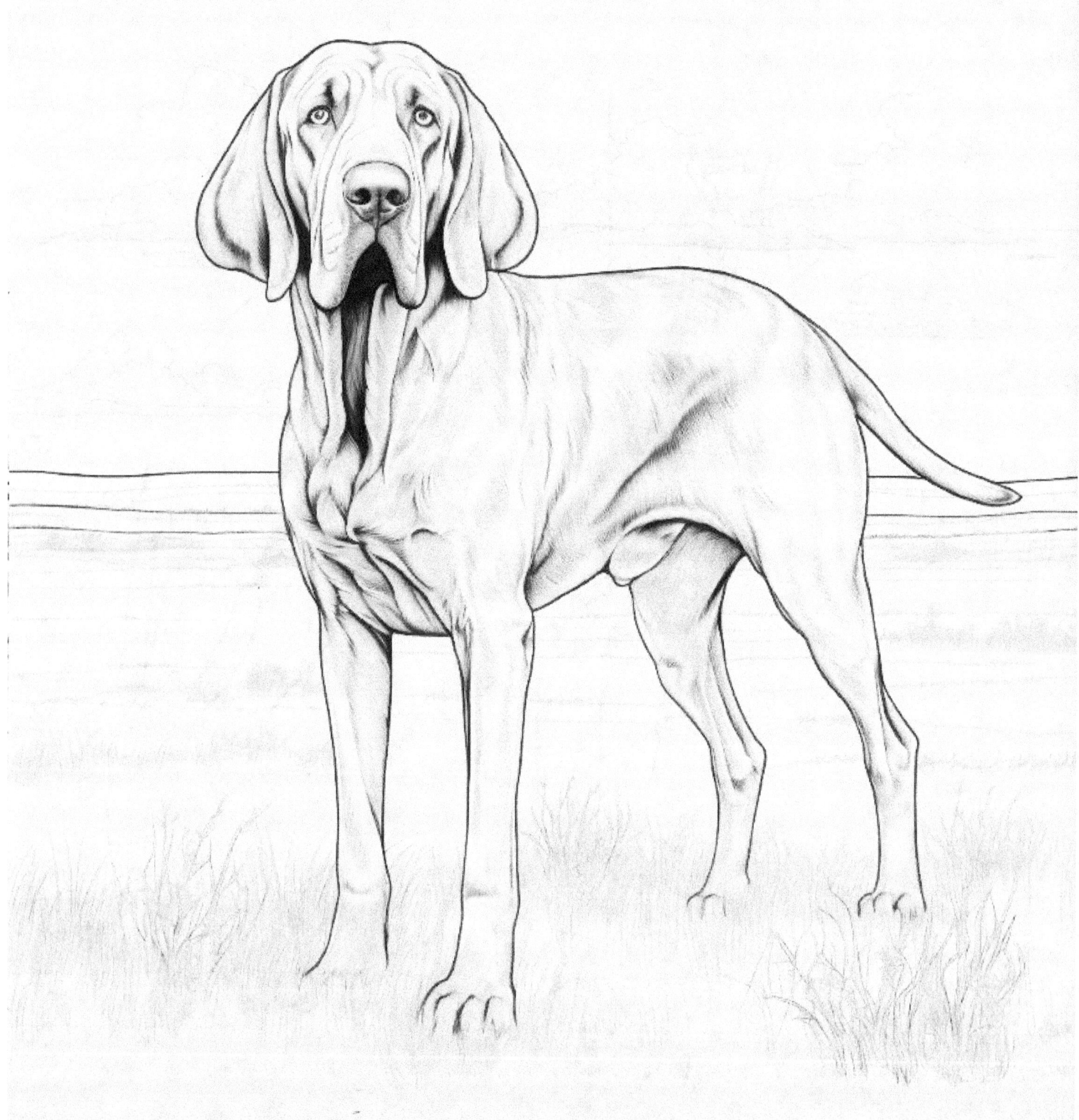

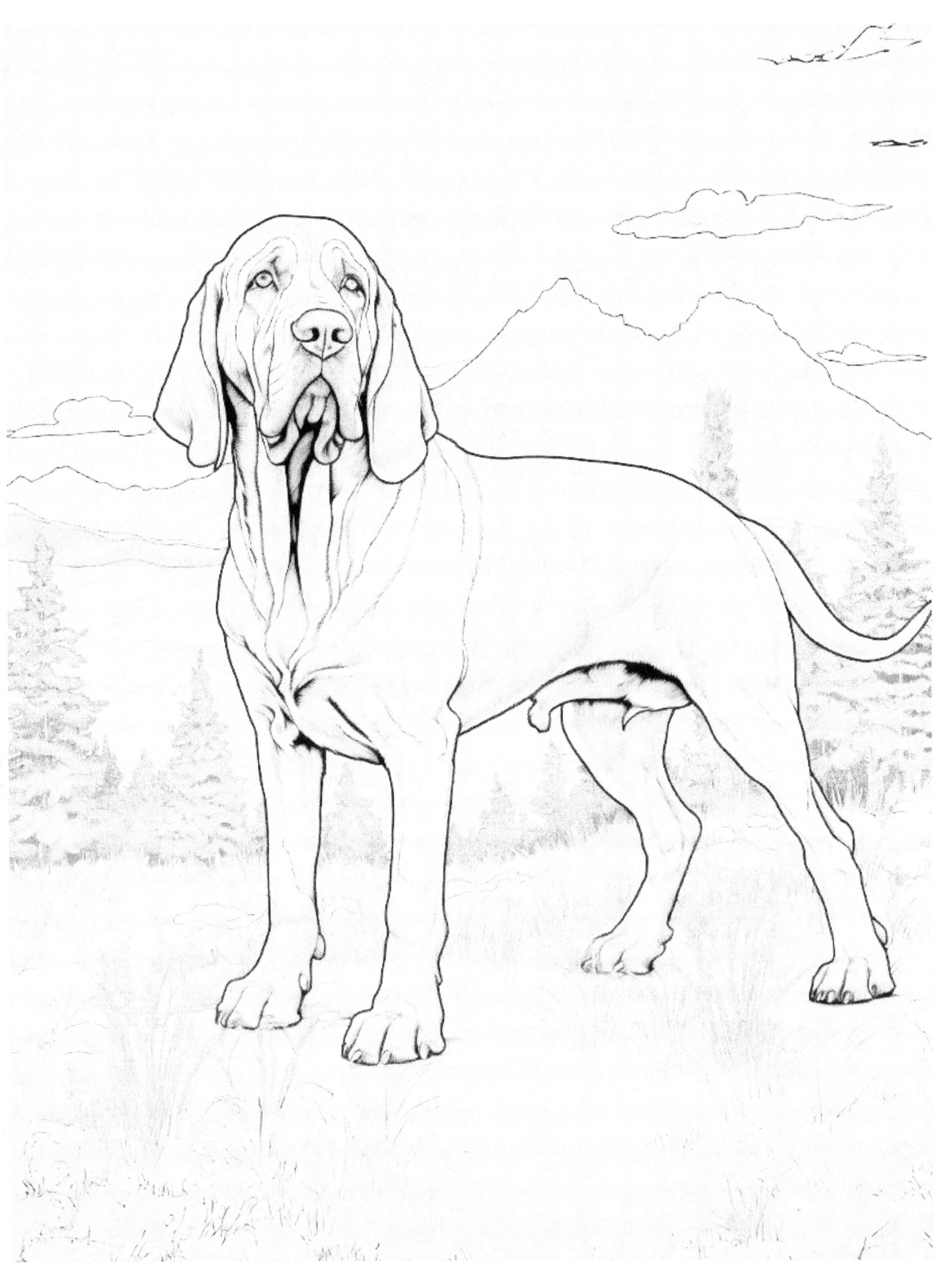

Thank You
For Being Part of Our Creative Journey!

To Our Dearest Customers,

We hope you've enjoyed every moment spent coloring the dogs in "Paws & Colors: A Dog Lover's Coloring Adventure." Your support means the world to us, and we're thrilled that our furry companions have brought joy to your creative world.

We invite you to continue exploring your artistic passions and discovering more of our creative offers at Department3C. Visit us at www.department3c.com to find a treasure trove of inspiring content, from coloring books, children's books, empowering coaching books, and MORE! There's something for everyone who seeks inspiration, relaxation, and personal growth.

Creativity knows no bounds, and our journey together is far from over. Stay connected, stay creative, and share your beautiful artwork. Creativity is a gift; we're grateful to be part of your artistic adventure.

Thank you again for choosing "Paws & Colors," until we meet again in the colorful art world, keep coloring, dreaming, and creating!

With heartfelt gratitude,
Severen Henderson
Founder, Department3C